Albert
EINSTEIN

GET ON FIRST NAME TERMS with some of the WORLD'S MOST AMAZING PEOPLE!

Elon — Technological powerhouse and innovator

Emmeline PANKHURST — Feisty women's rights campaigner

Amelia EARHART — High-flying feminist icon

Harry HOUDINI — Death-defying escape artist

Malala YOUSAFZAI — Teenage activist for girls' rights

Ada LOVELACE — The woman who made coding cool

Abraham LINCOLN — The man who abolished slavery in the US

Ferdinand MAGELLAN — Gifted, globetrotting Portuguese pioneer

Albert EINSTEIN — The most intelligent man who ever lived?

Beyoncé KNOWLES-CARTER — Superwoman and superstar

Nelson MANDELA — World-famous freedom fighter

first names

Albert
EINSTEIN

Haydn Kaye

Illustrations by Mike Smith

This book is dedicated with love to Amelia McCann

First Names: ALBERT EINSTEIN
is a
DAVID FICKLING BOOK

First published in Great Britain in 2021 by
David Fickling Books,
31 Beaumont Street,
Oxford, OX1 2NP

Text © Haydn Kaye, 2021
Illustrations © Mike Smith, 2021

978-1-78845-077-5

1 3 5 7 9 10 8 6 4 2

The right of Haydn Kaye and Mike Smith to be identified
as the author and illustrator of this work has been asserted
in accordance with the Copyright, Designs and Patents Act 1988.

All rights reserved. No part of this publication may be reproduced,
stored in a retrieval system, or transmitted in any form or by
any means, electronic, mechanical, photocopying, recording
or otherwise, without the prior permission of the publishers.

Papers used by David Fickling Books are from well-managed
forests and other responsible sources.

DAVID FICKLING BOOKS Reg. No. 8340307

A CIP catalogue record for this book is available from the British Library.

Printed and bound in Great Britain by Clays Ltd, Elcograf S.p.A

The facts in *First Names: Albert Einstein* have been carefully checked
and are accurate to the best of our knowledge, but if you spot
something you think may be incorrect please let us know.
Some of the passages in this book are actual quotes from Albert and
other important people. You'll be able to tell which ones they are by
the style of type: '*As long as there will be man, there will be war.*'

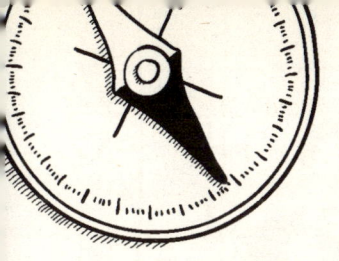

Contents

Introduction – Albert Is Awestruck	7
1 – Absent-Minded Albert	12
2 – Albert The Alien	21
3 – Albert Asks The Big Questions	30
4 – Albert And The Actual World	42
5 – Albert Aces It!	56
6 – Albert's 'Great Work Of Art'	70
7 – Albertmania!	87
8 – Albert Against The Nazis	103
9 – Albert Stays Awestruck	119
Timeline	134
Glossary	136
Index	138

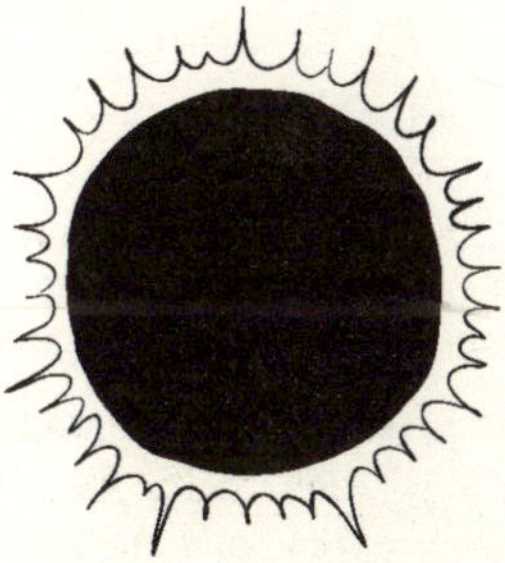

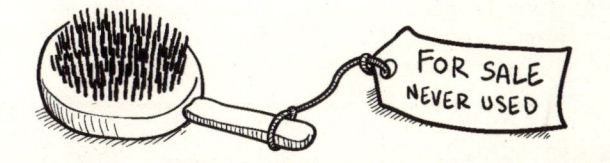

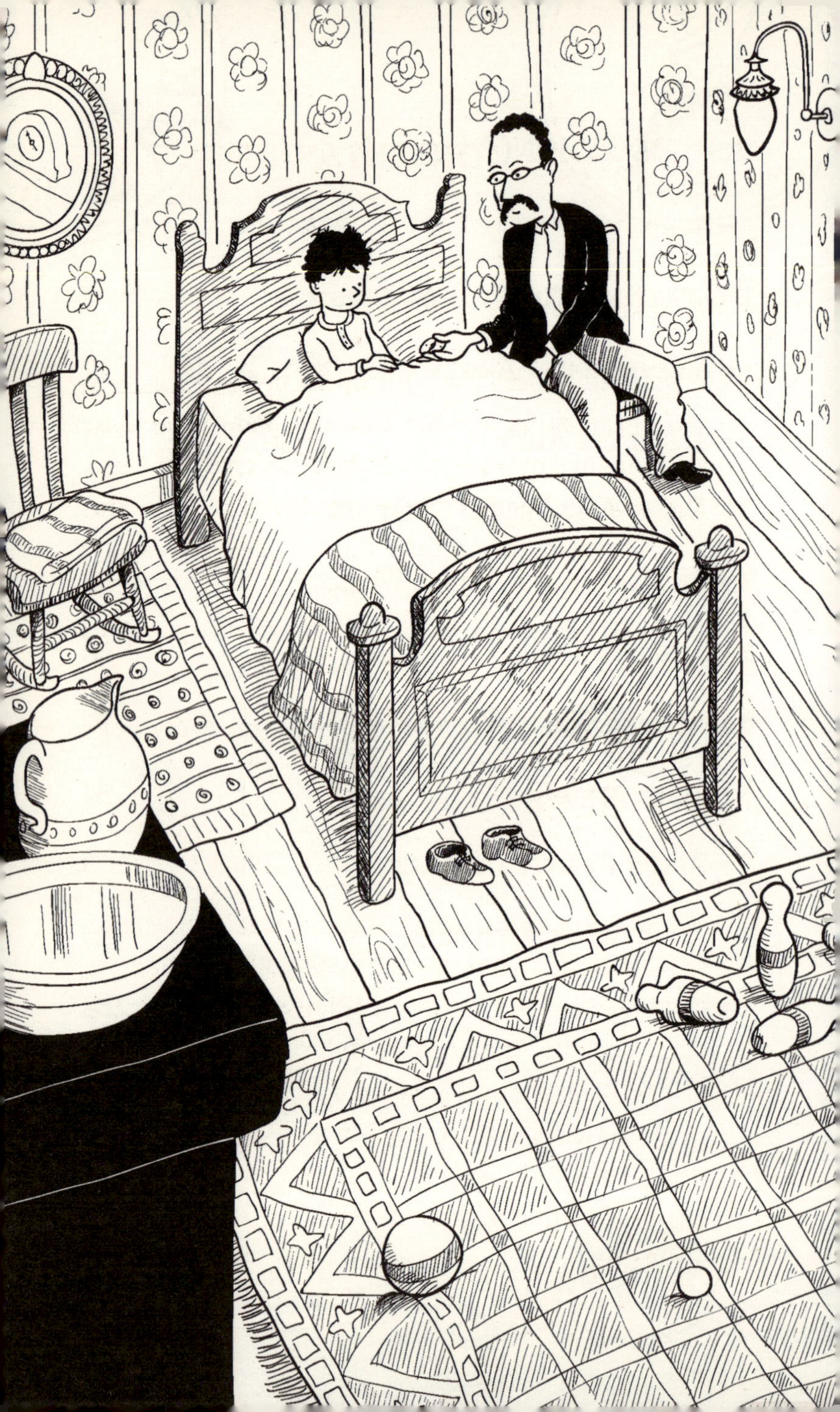

INTRODUCTION - ALBERT IS AWESTRUCK

THE PLACE: A posh family home in the city of Munich, Germany
THE TIME: 1884

Five-year-old Albert was laid up in bed with a bug. He wasn't making a fuss, but his dad wanted to cheer him up anyway. Albert had never been keen on the toys and games other kids loved back in the 1880s. He wasn't into sport either. So his dad brought him something else to keep him occupied.

It's magnetic. It always points to the North Pole.

Albert didn't know what his dad was talking about. And he'd never seen anything like this before. It looked like a clock, except instead of two hands there was just a needle. The needle didn't seem tightly fixed. It shivered a bit as it pointed dead ahead at the wall.

To get a closer look at it in the light, Albert gently turned the toy in his hands.

Then something peculiar happened.

When he moved it, the needle swung back to point dead ahead again. How come?

He turned the toy the other way. The needle swung briefly in the opposite direction, then once again ended up pointing ahead. The gadget in Albert's hands was, of course, a compass, and Albert was fascinated by it. Whichever way he turned it, something seemed to nudge the needle back.

Now, like the needle, Albert started shivering too. It had nothing to do with his illness. He was shivering out of **sheer excitement**. He couldn't touch the needle – it was out of reach behind thick glass – yet it moved all by itself. Scratching his head, and even a tiny bit scared, Albert looked all around the room. Something had to be making the needle point in just one direction. Something sort of ghostly, but so strong it couldn't be resisted. What exactly was this 'magnetic' power that always made the needle point to Earth's North Pole? What created it?

Little Albert had no answers yet, but there on his sickbed **he felt awestruck**, and it dawned on him that some seriously weird and wonderful stuff was going on. Stuff no one could see.

> There's more to life than meets the eye! How many other wonders might there be, hidden beyond the horizon, waiting to be discovered?

He never forgot that moment in his bedroom. When he was older he often talked about it, because this was the moment he got hooked on the mysteries of Earth and the heavens above. This was the moment his brain really began to whirr, and it went on whirring for the next 70 years.

WELCOME TO SPACETIME

Albert would go on to become the **world's most famous scientist** – ever. His ideas changed the way people thought about everything, from tiny atoms to the vast infinities of space. He was such a mega-genius that when he died in 1955 people did experiments on his brain, to try to see where his brilliant ideas came from!

Here are just a few things Albert went on to discover:

- 💡 Time runs at different speeds, depending on where you are and what you're doing. It even passes more slowly at your feet than it does at your head!

- 💡 Space is not just nothingness – it's actual stuff!

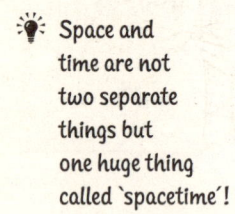

- 💡 Space and time are not two separate things but one huge thing called 'spacetime'!

> I'm not late, miss, I just got space and time mixed up.

Of course there's more to understand about these discoveries, and we'll be looking a bit harder at them later on, but here's a heads-up: don't expect it all to seem dead simple! During Albert's lifetime just about everyone who wasn't great at maths (from the US president down) was baffled by his super-smart ideas or 'theories'. Even top scientists were sometimes bewildered.

> You never really understand a new theory – you just get used to it!

To help you out, Albert himself has travelled back specially through spacetime to explain a few things. And here he is right now. Ladies and gentlemen, boys and girls, please say hello to the great, the one and only, *Professor Albert Einstein*!

> Oh, please, not 'Professor'. Just call me Albert.

Ok, Albert!

> And it's really not so important to follow the maths in my theories.

It's not?

> What matters most is **imagining** how things can be different. And I mean **all** things – not just in science, but in life too.

Right! Well, this is the story of *your* life, Albert. And all the absolutely incredible things that *you* imagined. So let's zoom back to where it all began . . .

1   ABSENT-MINDED ALBERT

With his angel face and big sad eyes, Albert made a cute five-year-old – the sort of child any parent would be proud of. And Albert's mum and dad *were* proud of him. They were proud of their daughter too, little Maja, who was a couple of years younger.

Young Maja was fine. She would chatter away happily all day long. But the Einsteins worried about big brother Albert because – well, he **hardly said a word**.

The few times Albert did speak, he'd try out the word or sentence first, whispering it to himself until he felt he had it right – which sounded slightly odd. Then, when he spoke the words out loud, they often sounded weird. For example, before his sister was born, his parents told him the new baby would be like an **amazing new toy**. Albert spent hours imagining this new toy. So when Maja finally arrived she was such a huge disappointment that Albert just looked at her and said, 'But where are the wheels?'

Albert's parents couldn't make him out. He wasn't like any of the other kids in the neighbourhood. His memory seemed hopeless, and because he always forgot to put his socks on in the morning and comb his hair, the family maid gave him a nickname: 'der Depperte'. That's German for the Dopey One. It sounds mean, but it's pretty much what everybody thought. Little Albert seemed to be **away with the fairies**.

Music Matters

Not everyone starts talking at the same age. It turned out Albert was just a late developer, and once he got properly chatty he showed how super-intelligent he was. But he didn't stop being a bit different. In spite of that tricky first meeting with Maja, he got on well with her, but mostly he just played on his own. He liked doing puzzles and making houses out of playing cards – some of them teetering up to 14 storeys high! But he had a **filthy temper:** once he hurled a chair at one of his tutors.

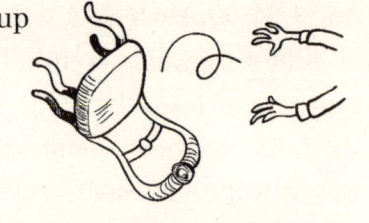

Albert's mum, Pauline, was a really good pianist and she loved music, so she arranged for Albert to have violin lessons.

Don't even think about it!

At first Albert didn't like being taught, but then he heard a brilliant violinist playing music written by another genius, Wolfgang Amadeus Mozart, and it blew him away. The sound was so beautiful, so pure, and yet **so wonderfully simple** that Albert could hardly believe his ears! After that, Albert practised like crazy until he could perform that same piece of music. Soon he was playing duets with his mum on the piano.

Albert carried on playing the violin for the rest of his life (and Mozart remained his #1 composer). But he didn't play just when he had a bit of downtime. Music meant a whole lot more to Albert than that. Once he was grown-up, whenever he hit a knotty scientific problem he'd pick up his violin and saw away in his kitchen late into the night. Then often he would stop playing and cry, 'I've got it!'

Later on, music inspired Albert to make scientific breakthroughs time after time. But it didn't work with any old music – there was one kind of music he hated with a passion.

During the 1880s, soldiers often passed through Munich, the city in Germany where Albert grew up. They'd march to pipes and drums and the local kids would rush out to watch them, then rush off to play war games themselves. But **little Albert never joined in**. Just thinking about war brought him out in a cold sweat. One day when the troops marched past, he burst into tears.

> When I grow up, I don't want to be one of those.
>
> But all our young men must serve in the German army when they turn 17.
>
> Left, right!
>
> Left, right!

While Albert felt sorry for the soldiers, because they'd have to risk their lives if war broke out, watching them also made him angry.

> *That a man can take pleasure in marching in formation to the strains of a band is enough to make me despise him.*

Albert didn't just hate the idea of war. He also hated taking orders – from anyone. And that included his schoolteachers.

Not A Very Happy Gym Bunny

By the time he started primary school, it was clear Albert *wasn't* dopey. He got great marks there, and when at the age of nine he moved on to the gymnasium (that's a German secondary school, by the way, not a place to get a six-pack) he continued to do well. But he was still seen as **a bit of a rebel**.

Pupils were expected to learn their lessons off by heart, which wasn't easy for Albert with his bad memory. The teachers tended to bark out facts and dates – and to Albert that felt like being in the army! So his attention would often wander, and that infuriated his teachers. They were irritated by his **all-round scruffiness** too. Here's what actually happened in one of his lessons:

> Einstein, get out of my class!
>
> But I haven't done anything wrong, sir!
>
> *No, but you sit there in the back row and smile, and your mere presence here undermines the respect of the class for me.*

Albert didn't really disrespect people in authority. But he'd already realized there was another way of learning – by **working out answers for himself**. That's what his uncle Jakob trained him to do when he dropped by Albert's family home and set him maths problems to solve. Then from the age of ten, with the help of a young student, Max Talmud, Albert began to learn even more . . .

How Albert Solved Max's Problems

The Einsteins lived in Germany so, not surprisingly, they were all German, but they were also Jewish. Centuries before Albert was born, Jews had lived in Palestine in the Middle East – where Israel and various Arab countries are today. But throughout history, millions of Jews had moved to Europe to live.

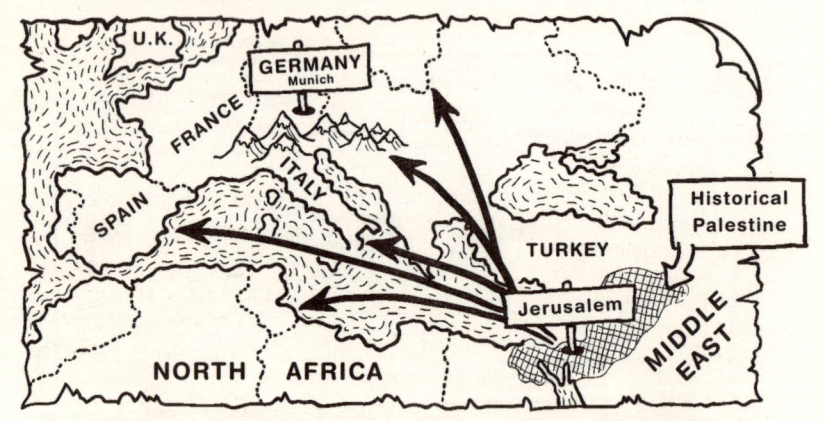

Often, the Jews fitted in really well. But sometimes

they were badly treated by the local Europeans, who were mostly Christians.

> These Jews are not the same as us. They've got their own religion and customs.

> But we all worship the same god!

> Yeah, but they're still different, and we don't like different.

One Jewish custom was to give a meal to a poor student on Saturdays, the Jewish holy day. Albert's parents didn't take these traditions too seriously, but for a few years they did invite Max Talmud, who was studying medicine, to eat with them on Thursdays.

Albert loved Max's visits. He'd bring science books about nature, volcanoes, stars – **all the fun stuff** Albert hardly ever got to hear about at school.

The needle in a compass is actually a little, lightweight magnet with a pointed end. Like all magnets, it has a north pole and a south pole, and like all magnets it will swivel towards the opposite pole of another magnet. The Earth itself is a gigantic magnet too – it's as if a great iron bar runs through its centre from top to bottom. Since the little pointed end of the magnet in the compass is always attracted to its opposite pole on the Earth, that means it always swivels in the direction of the North Pole.

> Oh, so **this** is how magnetism works!

> He understands so much but still can't use a comb!

Albert devoured the science books like comics, and Max also brought him geometry and maths problems to solve between his visits. Albert was fantastic at those, and soon the student couldn't keep up with the messy-haired teen.

> I just wanted to ask my own questions and find my own answers. I wanted to look **beyond the horizon** – where I sensed all the wonders were!

As Albert turned 15, life was starting to seem **extremely interesting**.

And that's precisely when everything took a sudden turn for the worse.

2   Albert The Alien

Albert's dad, Hermann, ran a firm producing electrical equipment with his brother, Albert's uncle Jakob. For a while that made them a good living, but Hermann wasn't the world's greatest businessman, and in 1894 the company went bust.

Hermann and Jakob decided the only way forward was to make **a fresh start** somewhere else, and they decided to move from Germany to Italy, taking their families with them. Just one person was going to be left behind.

The Dopey One Drops Out

While the Einstein clan made a sharp exit to Italy, Albert couldn't even stay on in his old Munich home. It was pulled down to make way for an apartment block! Albert was forced to move in with a distant relative and his spirits sank to an **all-time low**. Three more years of being barked at in school – he wasn't sure he could face it!

But as the 1894 Christmas holidays approached, he hit on a cunning plan. He went to see the family doctor, who happened to be Max Talmud's older brother. Albert really did feel awful, so the doctor signed him off school till he was better, but he had no intention of going back. Instead he packed his things and took a train to Italy.

In fact, Albert didn't just plan to stop going to school in Germany. His aim was to stop being German altogether! In just over a year he'd be 17. If he signed a load of papers saying he was no longer a German citizen, he could get out of doing military service.

It was win-win for me!

Out of school – and out of Germany – Albert heaved a deep sigh of relief. To get into Zurich Technical College, he didn't need a high-school diploma – he just had to pass the college's own tests. And after a friend of the Einsteins wrote to the Zurich professors explaining how 'gifted' Albert was, they let him take the tests two years early, when **he was still just 16**.

Before that day came, Albert revised hard on his own. He also dropped in on the occasional lecture at the University of Pavia – he wasn't a registered student but, like the family friend said, he was gifted so why shouldn't he? In his free time he travelled around Italy, taking in museums and art galleries. He often went hiking (probably with a handy compass to guide him). He even trekked across the mighty Alps to visit an uncle in Genoa, nearly 80 miles (129 km) away.

> Albert! You didn't **walk** eighty miles to see me, did you?!

> Of course not, uncle. I took the train for twenty!

Finally, in October 1895, Albert travelled to Zurich to take the college tests. He probably wasn't too nervous. For a young man with a brain the size of Albert's, **what could possibly go wrong**? His plan was to study engineering once he got in, just like his uncle Jakob before him. Then he would probably join the family firm.

But guess what?

Albert failed! Just being brilliant at maths and science subjects wasn't enough. It turned out he needed to be a whizz at subjects like French, zoology and botany too. And overall Albert just didn't come up to scratch.

That meant the Einsteins had to think again about Albert's future.

BACK TO SCHOOL - BUT THIS TIME NO BARKING

In the end, Albert's parents packed him off to a Swiss secondary school in Aarau, a small town 28 miles (46 km) outside Zurich. If he qualified for a diploma from there, he could apply for college in Zurich again.

So it was back to school for Albert. His heart must have been in his boots. But Aarau couldn't have been more unlike Albert's school in Germany, and Jost Winteler, who ran the place with his wife, shared Albert's views on education:

Love is a better teacher than duty.

Jost Winteler

My thoughts exactly.

Jost didn't believe in filling up his students with fact after boring fact. Instead he liked to point them in the right direction, then let them work out their own answers. Albert was soon enjoying one of the **best years of his life**. He even lived with the Winterlers, and was so relaxed in their home he started calling them 'Papa' and 'Mamerl'. And, for the first time ever, he actually made some friends his own age!

In 1896 Albert took his final exams and scored top or near-top marks in absolutely everything – except French. He never did get the hang of that.

He got his diploma, resat the technical college tests, and this time Zurich opened its doors wide to him. Albert was still six months too young, but no one was counting. It seemed this kid really was gifted!

Albert Peers Beyond The Horizon

Autumn 1896 was an exciting time for a clever teenager to be alive. Everywhere you looked, science was throwing up new inventions. Telephones! X-rays! Cinema films! Cars! And now that Albert had stopped being German, he was officially an 'alien', which meant he didn't need to do military service! For the next five years he was a citizen of nowhere, though he preferred to think of himself as a **citizen of the world**.

Meanwhile, things weren't going quite so well for the rest of the Einsteins. The family firm was struggling as much in Italy as it had in Germany. That put Albert right off becoming an engineer, and when he got to Zurich he decided to study maths instead, alongside the subject he would come to love above all others: physics.

Maths and physics wouldn't train him up for any particular job, but Albert described them both as 'thinking for its own sake'. And if there was one thing he loved, it was thinking. Or better still – imagining.

Albert had always thought in pictures rather than words – which might explain why he was so slow to talk. (And maybe no words existed yet for some of the visions in Albert's head!) But at the Wintelers' home, aged only 16, he really **got his imagination into gear** by carrying out what he called a 'thought experiment'.

Thought Experiment.

1. Sit down alone (or stand, or even play the violin).

2. Imagine riding alongside a beam of light.

3. Wonder what might happen.

Of course, in real life this would be impossible. Light travels at more than 670 million mph (that's 1,078 million km/h).

This would mean you could travel from the UK to Australia in one-nineteenth of a second!

4. But what if you **could** ride beside a light beam?

5. People say light travels in waves...

6. ...so would you be able to see the **front** of the wave beside you?

Good job I don't get travel sick!

Not all that many years later, thought experiments like this would help Albert to hit on theories that changed the way we think about space, time and reality! And unlike experimental scientists who can't work without labs and white coats and research teams, Albert needed no such equipment. Using data already gathered by other scientists, he could perform his own experiments even **sitting on a bus**!

> You see, it's all just a matter of using your imagination.

Well, it is if you happen to be a total genius!

> Ah, but **everyone** should think: 'What if?' It can help to change the world.

Really?

> Really! That's what the great geniuses of the past did. You should talk about them too, not just me. Too much of this story so far is merely personal.

Those guys are coming up, don't worry. But we love all this stuff about *you*, Albert. We want to know what really made you tick, so let's get back to Zurich . . .

3   Albert Asks The Big Questions

Over the next four years, Albert lived the dream in Zurich. Switzerland's biggest city was a fun place to be, and if you think he studied like crazy after all the trouble he had getting into the technical college, think again! Without his parents or the Wintelers to keep an eye on him, he discovered there was **far more to life** than books.

Albert loved nothing better than cutting lectures and hanging out in cafés. He'd guzzle iced coffee, smoke pipes and set the world to rights with his new student mates. He still played his violin, and now he had loads of concerts to go to as well. He even added a new open-air passion to his love of hiking: sailing on the Alpine lakes nearby.

Albert Becomes A Real Rebel

He didn't exactly neglect his studies, but Albert being Albert, he worked in his own way. He read masses about all the latest ideas in physics, then sat in cafés debating them. The trouble was, studying in Zurich was a bit like being back at school. There was **quite a lot of barking** from the staff, and the students had to do a lot of learning by heart.

The professors were all top men (no such thing as women professors back then), and Albert had expected them to inspire him. But they seemed more interested in old explanations of how the universe worked, instead of exploring new ones. Albert didn't rate two of his teachers in particular – Jean Pernet and Heinrich Weber – and he didn't hide how he felt.

> You always do something different from what I have ordered, when you bother to turn up at all!

> *You're a very clever boy, Einstein. But you have one great fault: you'll never let yourself be told anything!*

> And don't keep calling me Mr Weber! My proper title is Professor!

> Yes, Mr Weber.

Winding up his teachers was a good laugh, but one day Albert would find it hadn't been such a good idea to make an enemy out of Heinrich Weber. Meanwhile he had two sets of exams to pass before he left college and started to earn a living.

Now Albert was brilliant, no question. But the first set of exams, two years in, were based on what students had learned in class – **classes Albert usually cut**. It was lucky, then, that one of his new friends happened to be absolutely amazing at maths.

Marcel Grossmann didn't just have a perfect attendance record – he'd taken detailed notes of every lesson too, and he didn't mind sharing them with Albert. The pair of them spent the summer of 1898 getting up to speed for the exam – and when the results were posted, Albert came out top of the class, with Marcel in second place.

Marcel wasn't really miffed. He'd already told his parents that Albert was 'someone who will one day be great'. Not everyone agreed, however.

Albert still hadn't grown out of his old absent-mindedness, and it seemed the deeper he got into physics, and wondering about the true nature of space and time, the less clued-up he was about everything else. He was forever getting his landlady out of bed to let him in because he'd **left his key in his room**. Once, after staying over at a friend's house, he said goodbye in the morning and left without his suitcase.

However forgetful Albert was, his friends still loved him. It didn't put the girls off either. For them, he was dreamy in more ways than one! (And Albert was always the life and soul of the party.)

He loved the girls right back as well. There was one girl in particular . . .

WHEN JOHNNIE MET DOLLIE

Back in Aarau, Albert had got friendly with the Wintelers' daughter, Marie. They'd played musical duets together and been on bird-watching trips in the woods. But life in Zurich was such a blast, Albert's interest in Marie cooled – though he kept sending her his **dirty laundry**, which she lovingly kept washing and mailing back to him!

> Something nice from Albert, dear?

By now Albert had spotted a young woman called Mileva Marić, who came from Serbia in southern Europe. She was studying physics at Zurich too. Back then **very few women** went to college, let alone studied physics, so she must have stood out. The friendlier Albert got with her, the cleverer he realized she was – and she worked at her studies as if there was no tomorrow too! Meanwhile he had iced coffee to drink, pipes to smoke and professors to wind up.

In summer 1897 they went hiking together. Mileva also played the piano – so a new duet team was soon born – and Albert really liked the sweet way she sang.

> But most of all I liked the way we talked deeply about whatever books we were reading.

Mileva shared Albert's fascination with stuff like the compass needle always pointing north, and what might happen if you travelled next to a light wave. He'd never stopped being awestruck by this sort of thing, and it thrilled him that Mileva wasn't afraid to tell him her own ideas, even when she disagreed with him.

> Something deeply hidden has to lie behind it all. Something wonderful. Something as harmonious as the music of Mozart. I plan to find what it is!

> And I can help you!

Albert and Mileva got together because of their love of physics, but it wasn't long before they **fell in love** with each other. As Johannzel (Johnnie) and Doxerl (Dollie), they wrote funny loving letters to each other. 'Johnnie' even wrote a weird poem for his 'Dollie':

> *Oh my! That Johnnie boy!*
> *So crazy with desire,*
> *While thinking of his Dollie*
> *His pillow catches fire.*

> Oh, **Johnnie!**

> I don't see anything weird at all about that poem!

The Lovebirds Look To The Future

The course of true love does not always run smooth, however, and Albert was disappointed to find Mileva wasn't quite such a hit with his friends.

In those days, women weren't expected to show they had brains; they were generally invited along to look nice and say very little, and Albert's mates found Mileva hard work. As for his mum and dad, they were horrified at the thought of 'losing' their only son to her. They simply didn't believe she could make Albert happy, and they picked holes in the relationship from the start. They especially didn't like the fact that Mileva was three years older than Albert, or that she seemed to come from a less posh family than the Einsteins. She wasn't even Jewish like them!

Albert's parents found Mileva **unsuitable in every way**. They even criticized her height! Albert himself was only 5 feet 8 (172 cm), and Mileva barely came up to his shoulder. But Albert had never let anyone tell him what to think, say or do. *'In short,'* he wrote to his sweetheart, *'without you, my life is no life.'*

Albert and Mileva wanted to be together for ever. Once they'd got their diplomas, they would both be qualified to teach in a secondary school, but no way did Albert plan to wind up barking at bunches of bored pupils.

He just had to go on asking the big questions, sorting out how the universe really worked – and to fund his research, **he'd need a job** as an assistant to a college professor. Since Albert had been such an alpha student, he'd surely be able to pick his post. Then as soon as he was making some money, he and Mileva could set a date for their wedding.

> And what will *I* do in the future, Johnnie?

> I thought you'd have our children, Dollie, and take care of our home.

> Er...

> Or maybe we could work **together** as professional physicists!

Reality Check

First, though, in 1900, they had to take their second and last set of Zurich exams.

Albert put in just enough effort to get his diploma. His exam results **weren't earth-shattering**, but he got his pass and became a graduate. Mileva, however, didn't.

Now failing exams can happen to the best of people (as Albert well knew). Mileva's mood nonetheless hit rock bottom. She wanted to quit studying for ever, but Albert talked her into having another shot at the exam the next year. Everything could still be fine, he told her, soon they would be working together, and one day money would be *'as plentiful as manure!'* But while Mileva was getting her qualification, he would find a professor to assist, then start his research. And who better to assist than their very own professor at Zurich – Heinrich Weber?

In went Albert's application. Back came Mr Weber's reply. It wasn't a yes!

This is what came of being such an annoying student. Still, there were plenty more professors, all over Europe, and **for 18 months** Albert applied to one after another after another – and every single time he drew a blank!

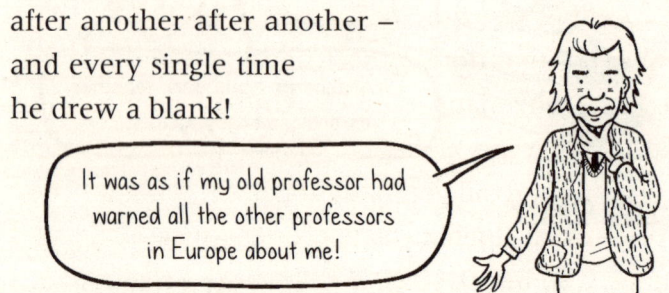

> It was as if my old professor had warned all the other professors in Europe about me!

Or maybe something more sinister was going on. Did Albert keep getting rejected because he was Jewish? He lived in worrying times, when people could be hateful to Jews for no reason whatever.

In 1901, and not in perfect health, Mileva **flunked her final exam** again. By then the couple were finding it hard to make ends meet, so to bring in a little cash, Albert bit the bullet and advertised his services as a private teacher:

> **Private Lessons**
> in
> Mathematics and Physics. Given most thoroughly by Albert Einstein Holder of the Technical College Teacher's Diploma
>
> Trial Lessons Free!

But it wasn't enough. Things were going so badly wrong that Mileva felt forced to spend some time back at home with her parents while Albert decided to try his luck in a new Swiss city, Bern. He had some connections there and hoped his job prospects might be better. But, **too poor to eat properly**, he developed stomach problems that would plague him for the rest of his life.

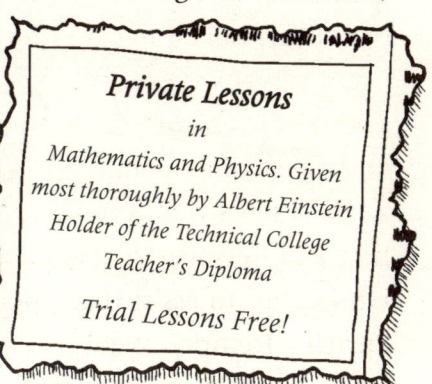

On a positive note, Albert had made another big decision. Switzerland was his kind of country. For hundreds of years it hadn't fought in a war – and the people there all got along together, whether they spoke German, French, Italian or the local language, Romansh. So in early 1901, just before he turned 22, Albert successfully applied to become a Swiss citizen.

Throughout this testing time, Albert's mum and dad weren't much use to him. His dad had fallen ill as his business crashed once again – and both his parents were as spiteful as ever about Mileva – but Albert did his best to keep her spirits up by letter.

Can you imagine how pleasant it will be when we're able to work together, completely undisturbed, and with no one around to tell us what to do?

Albert still dreamed they'd be able to do research together, looking beyond the horizon to unlock the hidden secrets of the universe. Then they would really make that 'Mr' Weber respect the name of Einstein – along with all the other **miserable professors** who hadn't wanted him as their assistant!

But by the middle of 1902, many top scientists were starting to doubt that there *were* any more secrets to be discovered. Here's what one of them is reported to have said shortly beforehand.

British Association for the Advancement of Science, 1900

There is nothing new to be discovered in physics now. All that remains is more and more precise measurement.

LORD KELVIN

Try telling that to the lonely young man in Bern with the grumbly tum!

But how could Albert prove that the experts were all wrong, and he was right to keep asking those big questions? Without a regular income he couldn't afford the rent, let alone sort out how the universe worked, and he certainly couldn't think about marriage and a family.

What Albert needed was for someone to come along and wave a magic wand to **solve all his problems**. Funnily enough, that's pretty much what happened!

4   Albert And The Actual World

Here's Albert, grappling with a knotty problem at his brand-new place of work. You'll notice he isn't wearing the white lab coat of a regular scientific researcher. That's because the job he landed in Bern in 1902 was not in any sort of university.

Having totally failed to find a professor he could assist, Albert was saved from starvation when his good friend, Marcel Grossmann, stepped in. Marcel didn't exactly wave a magic wand, but he did **pull some strings** to get Albert a post as a 'technical expert – class three' at the Federal Office for Intellectual Property. Most people just called it the Patent Office.

The job paid 3,500 Swiss francs a year.

> Which was more than I'd have earned as a junior professor!

So just what did he have to do for eight hours a day, six days a week, to earn this hugely welcome salary?

'THINK OF EVERYTHING AS WRONG!'

Patent offices still exist all over the world, and when you dream up a brilliant idea for a brand-new product (a combined lawnmower and hairdryer perhaps?), this is the place you need to run it past.

If the experts at the Patent Office decide no one has come up with your idea before – and it looks as if it might work – they give you a 'patent' for it. This means only you are allowed to make or sell and profit from the product for an agreed period. (When that period's up, everyone else can try to make a fortune out of it.)

Albert was one of these experts at the Patent Office in Bern city centre. His boss, Mr Haller, was very strict. Before an official patent was handed out, he'd get his workers to investigate each new application very, very thoroughly.

When you pick up an application, think everything the inventor says is wrong!

Albert was just fine with that. As a rebel and a bit of a bad boy, he'd always questioned everything anyway: this was his whole way of working!

What's more, with a regular salary, he could afford to marry Mileva. At Bern registry office on 6th January 1903 they finally **tied the knot**. Only two guests witnessed the event – Albert's friends Conrad Habicht and Maurice Solovine. After a small celebration, Albert and Mileva returned to their new flat, where some things never changed:

Now where did I put my keys?

Albert's dad had at last accepted Mileva into the family, but sadly he died three months before the wedding. None of Albert's other relatives came to celebrate with them. Life went on, however, and the next year a new little Einstein was hatched: Hans Albert. He was followed, in 1910, by a second son, Eduard, better known by the nickname 'Tete'.

The boys thrilled Albert, although – like most dads back then – he didn't spend masses of time with them. He did knock together some great toys for little Hans Albert, though.

And here comes the cable car.

So now Albert had some serious responsibilities: a job to keep and a family to care for. They weren't living in the lap of luxury – 3,500 Swiss francs went only so far – but they did have a roof over their heads and enough food to eat.

> I really do think that's enough of this merely personal stuff now. I had much bigger things on my mind too. You make it sound as if I'd given up on physics!

As if! Hold on tight, the physics is coming right up . . .

Eight Hours Of Mischief

For all his absent-mindedness, Albert knew how to organize his time. He spent eight hours a day at the office (sometimes secretly doing his own research there), and he slept for eight hours too. But since, like most mums in the early 1900s, Mileva did almost all the childcare and housework, this left Albert **eight hours for other activities** – including what he liked to call 'mischief'.

After all his bad luck with teachers, Albert decided to start teaching himself – studying to become a doctor in physics, while also publishing scientific articles, or 'papers', on what he was reading and thinking about.

> I won't make myself learn anything off by heart! And I'll **never** bark at myself!

> I might bark at you, though!

Albert used to bounce his ideas off Mileva, but he didn't do that so much now. More often he met up with three physics-mad friends who lived close by: Conrad and Maurice, the witnesses at his wedding, and his best friend of all, Michele Besso. They jokingly called themselves **the Olympia Academy**. Michele also worked at the Patent Office from 1904 – so Albert was able to debate physics with him while they walked to and from work.

Albert used his three friends like a kind of think tank. But the most important work still went on inside his own head, because he continued to think – very hard – in pictures, and even a genius finds it difficult to *talk* in pictures to another person.

So what was Albert thinking so hard about?

The answer is pretty much the same stuff that had been obsessing him since he was a small kid. In other words – this wonderful world of ours, everything in it, and everything beyond it. Or to put it another way: reality. But what exactly is reality?

> Doh! It's what we see right in front of us!

Hmm, yes and no to that.

Sometimes a genius will come along and show us that what we've **always believed** to be reality – well, isn't reality. In ancient Greek times, more than 2,000 years ago, this happened quite a lot. Brainy ancient Greeks came up with all these gobsmacking theories:

> Psst! The Earth is round and it floats in the sky.

> Rainwater comes from water on Earth that has evaporated to form clouds.

> Everything is made up of tiny atoms buzzing around, all pushing and pulling.

> But we can see the Earth is flat!

> And rainwater doesn't go up – it comes **down** from the sky!

> And where are these atoms you're talking about?

These new theories all sounded nuts, but each of them was right! Reality is *not* always what it seems, but sometimes it takes a great genius (who is also a bit of a rebel, like Albert) to come along and point it out. Their job is to look hard, think hard, and work out what they believe is the truth.

> It may then take hundreds of years for all of us to accept a theory. But when we finally do, we start to look at the world in a whole new way.

Hey, Albert! Why don't you tell us about some of these great geniuses?

> I'd love to. And then it'll be easier to make sense of what I myself was trying to do later on.

ALBERT EXPLAINS: TWO GREAT SCIENCE GENIUSES

> These two geniuses lived long before my time, but they felt like friends to me.

They were like giants too, because they could see (with their minds) much deeper and further than anyone else.

> Compared to them, I felt tiny, until I realized that if I stood on their shoulders, I could see even further than they had!

So here are the amazing things they pointed out:

Five hundred years ago, just about everyone believed the Sun went around the Earth. Then up popped Nicolaus Copernicus:

> Actually, it's the Earth that goes around the Sun.

> And he was right! But not everyone wanted to believe him.

Then, in the next century, along came Isaac Newton:

> All through the universe the force of 'gravity' makes every object attract every other object, even over great distances.

> It makes the Sun attract the Earth and the Earth attract the Moon. As a result, the entire heavens run like clockwork.

> Don't listen to him! He's mad!

> To most people this sounded crazy. (How could enormous great planets 'attract' one another?) But Newton had got it right!

> My office was tidier!

> I rated my friend Newton so highly, I kept a picture of him pinned above my desk!

Even today, it's hard to explain *why* these two great geniuses were right. That would involve some quite tricky sums. (Maths happens to be the best language for understanding and describing how the universe works.)

> But as I keep saying: to understand the importance of these theories, **you don't need to follow the sums!** If it's a good theory, it should be possible to explain it to a child! So I hope you won't be including any equations in this book.

Actually, Albert, there will be just one.

> Oh yes?

The most famous equation of all time – and it was dreamed up by you!

> Hmph, well, maybe just that one then!

Now when Albert was a student, one theory really fired him up. It was the theory of **electric and magnetic forces**, and it was based on the work of two geniuses a little closer in time to himself.

Good Vibrations

People had known about magnets and electricity for centuries – or at least they thought they had.

💡 In China, centuries ago, people used magnets to line up graves, thinking it would help dead spirits to walk into the afterlife.

Left a bit.

💡 In ancient Greece people noticed that rubbing amber created an 'electric charge', and this attracted bits of straw.

RUB RUB

Fancy that!

But it wasn't until the 1800s that two Brits sorted out how magnetic or electrical *forces* hold all solid objects together. First, Michael Faraday claimed that the 'space' around us isn't truly empty.

It's actually filled with a kind of massive, invisible cobweb that's held together by incredibly thin lines of force.

Carrying electric and magnetic forces from one object to another.

Altogether, they form what we now call electric and magnetic fields.

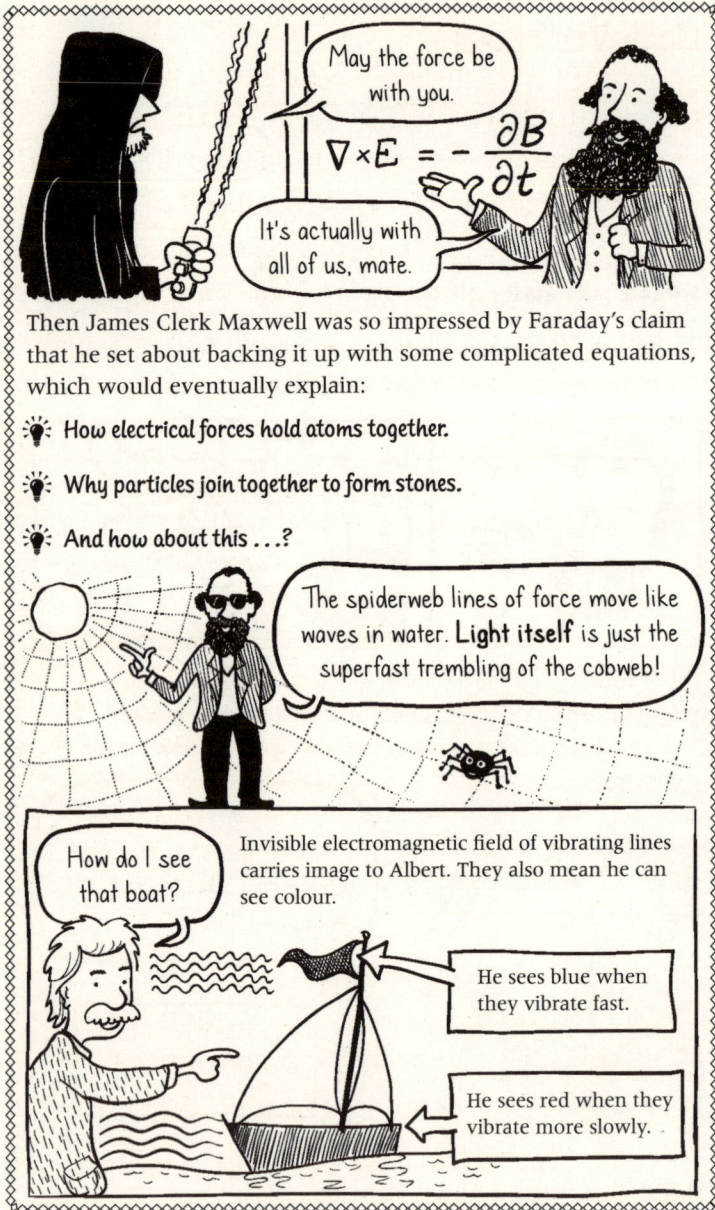

Then James Clerk Maxwell was so impressed by Faraday's claim that he set about backing it up with some complicated equations, which would eventually explain:

- 💡 How electrical forces hold atoms together.
- 💡 Why particles join together to form stones.
- 💡 And how about this...?

Faraday died in 1867, Maxwell in 1879. Without their brilliant work on electromagnetism, we wouldn't have ended up with lots of today's technology, like radio, TV, computers, satellites, Wi-Fi and the internet. So you can see why they excited Albert. He believed he could use their work to make **new discoveries** of his own. Because, although some scientists believed it was 'game over' for physics (see p. 40), Albert had a hunch we still knew only a fraction of the truth about space and time.

> Nature shows us only the tail of the lion, but I have no doubt that the rest of the lion is there, even if he can't reveal himself all at once. We see that lion only the way that a louse sitting on him would!

Luckily for the rest of us, Albert was a very clever louse indeed.

For years people had been noticing how bright he was (if also a bit absent-minded, and even – if you were a teacher – a wee bit annoying). But as Albert turned 26, he was about to prove to the world just what an **all-time genius** he really was.

5 Albert Aces It!

All Albert's reading, thinking and debating about physics gave him some **incredible ideas** of his own. But they usually didn't occur to him out of the blue.

> There was more to it than just thinking for a bit then snapping my fingers!

Often he had to work away like mad before he had a brainwave. Then he had to let other scientists know all about it. So he'd write up his ideas, and get them published as papers in *Annalen der Physik* – that's German for *Yearbook of Physics*.

Without TV, the internet and social media, news didn't get around anything like as fast as it does today. But during 1905 people were already starting to ask: 'Who is this guy from Bern, with all the amazing ideas?'

One of Europe's top physicists, Professor Max Planck, sent his own brilliant young assistant, Max von Laue, to find out. Turning up at the Patent Office, having found no one called Einstein at Bern

University, Max was told to follow the corridor, and Albert would come out to meet him. But when Albert came shuffling along, Max **walked straight past him**. How could a scruff like that be the genius everyone was talking about? Albert was shuffling back down the corridor by the time Max figured out who he was! But once the pair started talking physics, they hardly stopped for the rest of their lives.

> I'm sure you can be untidy, absent-minded **and** a great scientist!

Here are just two of the ideas Albert dropped on Max and the rest of the world during 1905 – which turned out to be Albert's big, big year.

Idea #1: Small Is Beautiful

The theory that all objects are made of atoms dates back to the ancient Greeks, but even in 1905 (2,300 years later) not everyone thought it had been proved.

It was a really nice *idea*, but did atoms actually exist? A great physicist of Albert's day said:

Have you ever seen an atom?

Ernst Mach

Nope, nothing here.

Of course, no one had. Atoms are so incredibly small, it's **impossible to see them** with the naked eye, or even under a microscope. If you put a trillion atoms in a line, they'd measure just one centimetre! So how could Albert prove they really are there?

Well, he looked at a speck of dust suspended in liquid. He watched as it trembled and lurched about in a weird little dance called 'Brownian motion' (after a scientist called Robert Brown who described it in the 1800s).

This is actually making me seasick!

Why does the speck jiggle about? Because it's being whacked by individual 'molecules' of air inside the liquid, colliding with it from all directions. Molecules aren't as small as atoms. We still can't see them, but it takes two or more atoms to make a molecule.

> Two oxygen atoms make up a molecule called O^2, which is in the air we all breathe. Three oxygen atoms make up O^3, which is a gas called ozone, that has a funny smell.

Albert watched the speck's movement very, very closely. Then he started doing some sums, and he worked out from the amount of movement how big the molecules whacking it had to be. From there, though it **sounds unbelievable**, he also calculated how big the individual atoms in a molecule were!

Helped along by Albert's idea, people had to agree that all objects and living things *are* made of atoms: gases, liquids, solid objects – *everything*.

> Inside gases, atoms and molecules swarm about loosely, so gases flow easily.

> They're more tightly packed in liquids.

> Molecules can hardly move at all in solid objects. And that includes you and me!

Idea #2: Prizewinning Particles

Albert's second big idea from 1905 is maybe even more amazing. It came to be known as the Law of the Photoelectric Effect, and one day he would get a very big prize for it.

Very basically, here's what it says:

> It's not just objects and living things that are made up of teeny-tiny particles all thrashing about. So is light!

> Gah!

How in all the universe did Albert work *that* out? In fact, it was an idea Professor Planck (see p. 56) had been playing around with already. For ages people had thought light moved in big waves. But the results of Prof. Planck's experiments had given him an idea:

Now Albert's investigations told him the prof's hunch was correct.

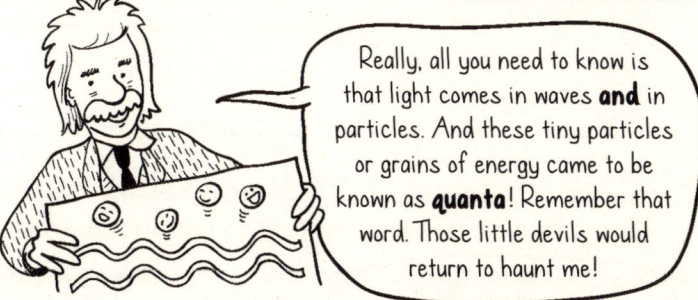

So those two 1905 ideas were absolute belters. But now we come to Albert's **most staggering bombshell of all** during his mega year. His Special Theory of Relativity!

This paper was only 30 pages long, and it only took him five weeks to write, although he'd had the idea on the boil for years. But, boy, did it pack a punch!

This was the idea that would make Albert a worldwide legend – and not just among scientists. It was about space and it was about time, and once people got to hear about it, they would never be able to think about either space or time in quite the same way ever again.

So what was the big idea then, Albert?

ALBERT EXPLAINS:
HIS THEORY OF RELATIVITY
Some of the things we take for granted turn out not to be true!
For example, the world feels flat and still.
But actually the Earth is continually spinning at 1,040 miles per hour, and orbiting the Sun at over 67,000 mph.
Woo-hoo!
1,040 miles = 1,674 km
67,000 mph = 107,000 km/h

These are true facts, but they took a long time to catch on. People still struggle to get their heads around them. Now what I'm about to tell you blew quite a lot of minds in 1905, and it still blows quite a few minds today! Are you ready?

Here is what my Special Theory of Relativity boils down to:

- **THERE IS ACTUALLY NO SUCH THING AS NOW. 'THE PRESENT' DOES NOT EXIST.**

- **THERE'S NO SINGLE TICK-TOCK EVERYWHERE IN OUR VAST UNIVERSE THAT WE CAN CALL TIME!**

Here's how you probably think about time as you sit reading this book.

PAST — PRESENT — FUTURE

I discovered there's a sort of twilight zone between the past and the future of any event. Not just the present, but a kind of str–et–ch–ed–out version of the present, which can last for more than just a moment.

This is how it works:

Try imagining you are calling a Martian from your bedroom.

> Hello?

Message takes 15 minutes to reach Mars.

> Qzkfy!

So the twilight zone here lasts for 15 minutes. The whole of this 15 minutes is 'now' – it isn't in the past or the future!

But the universe is gigantic. A 'light year' is the distance that light travels in a single Earth year, and the nearest galaxy to our Milky Way, the Andromeda Galaxy, is two and a half million light years away. This means the twilight zone of 'now' lasts for two and a half million years. That's two and a half million years when everything that happens there is neither in *our* past, nor in our future. It's all . . . RELATIVE!

> So I suggested we should stop thinking about space and time within the universe as separate things.

> Instead we might knit them together to form a bigger, more wonderful SPACETIME! (Just as the electric field and the magnetic field might merge into a single ELECTROMAGNETIC one.)

> So we can't say events are happening 'now' across the universe? But we can say 'here and now'?

> I **told** you a child could understand this!

And that's the gist of Albert Einstein's Special Theory of Relativity. It's called 'Special' because it only works under certain special conditions, when objects are moving in certain ways and at certain speeds. Later on, Albert came up with a more general theory, which is actually **easier to understand** – and that'll be in the next chapter.

But first let's take a look at something else Albert dreamed up in another 1905 paper. We warned you this was coming. Yes, it's time for . . .

The World's Most Famous Equation!

Even if we don't know what it means, lots of us have heard of $E=mc^2$. (That '^{2}' is just a maths way of saying a number must be 'squared' – or multiplied by itself, e.g. 5 squared = 5 x 5 = 25.) This dead famous equation has even had pop songs written about it.

So what was the equation about?

Albert was phenomenal at linking things up (things like electric and magnetic fields, or space and time). Now he wondered if the mass or weightiness of an object and the energy inside it might be two forms of the same thing. And – you guessed it – he found they were!

This meant that, under the right conditions, pure mass could be converted into pure energy (and vice versa). And we're not just talking about *a bit of energy* here. Take a single raisin, for example. The mass of that raisin is, in fact, **a vast amount of energy** all crammed in together. So what if you found a way to *un-cram* all the energy again?

One raisin x the speed of light x the speed of light again = about enough energy to power New York City for a day'!

Ok, so here is how my equation fits together.

$$E = mc^2$$

ENERGY — MASS — SPEED OF LIGHT — MULTIPLY THE SPEED OF LIGHT BY ITSELF

So ENERGY equals MASS multiplied by the speed of light, and then multiplied by the speed of light again!

Ta-da!

I'm not sure I want that much energy in my hand!

Such a lot of stored-up energy could maybe one day be tapped and put to good uses – such as providing power, the way electricity and gas do – and that would have been fine by Albert. Or maybe, just maybe, it might do the last thing he would ever have wanted: **cause mass destruction**.

We'll be coming back to this – big time.

Doctor In Demand

Albert wasn't even a researcher when he worked all this out. He was still at the Patent Office, and coming up with his theories during his eight hours of 'mischief' a day.

In 1905, using those eight hours, he'd qualified to be a doctor, but not a medical one. He wrote a long paper or 'thesis', which the University of Zurich approved, so now Albert could call himself 'Dr' Einstein. His thesis was on the subject of molecules, and though it wasn't as awesome as his other 1905 papers, it's **been really useful ever since** to people doing all sorts of stuff from cement-mixing to making aerosols.

Albert enjoyed his time at the Patent Office, but as news spread about his theories, job offers from colleges came tumbling in.

It **so** didn't matter what Mr Weber wrote about me after that!

Finally, in 1909, it was time for Albert to move on.

For the next four years Albert's little family **hardly had time to unpack** their suitcases. First Albert took a job at Zurich University. Then in 1911 he was offered the impressive-sounding post of Professor of Theoretical Physics at the German University in Prague (which is now in the Czech Republic, confusingly). And in 1912 he bounced back to Zurich, still as a Professor of Theoretical Physics, but now at the Federal Institute of Technology (his own old technical college had been upgraded)!

During these whirlwind years, Albert worked flat out to produce more theories, publishing paper after paper. (In the whole of his career, he published more than 300!) That didn't leave much time for the 'merely personal' part of his life.

He'd had two young sons around the house since 1910, and they took a lot of looking after. But Mileva suffered from rheumatism, and often struggled to keep the Einstein show on the road, so Albert sometimes had to play the violin to the kids to keep them quiet!

It could all get pretty hectic. Albert didn't always remember to wash; and he'd seldom taken much care over his clothes. A visiting student once found him in his study trying to work, scribbling equations with one hand and holding little Tete with the other. Meanwhile Hans Albert was playing on the floor with toy bricks and pestering his dad to join him. Albert just passed the baby to his student, then went on writing.

> Hold on a minute, I think I've nearly cracked this . . .

Young Einstein

Albert could have done with some better working conditions! At times all the stress really got to him. But his powers of concentration were amazing, and slowly but surely they were taking him closer to a **truly enormous breakthrough**: one that another world-famous scientist, Professor Paul Dirac, would say was probably the greatest scientific discovery ever made.

6 Albert's 'Great Work Of Art'

Towards the end of 1913 Albert became a German again. He had to: it was the only way he could take up a **fabulous new job** in Berlin, Germany's capital city. Berlin happened to be the world's leading centre for scientific research at the time, and Albert hadn't just been offered one new job there, he'd been offered *three*:

I hung on to my Swiss citizenship too, just in case!

Professor at University of Berlin | Director of new Physics Institute | Paid member of Prussian Academy of Sciences

Mileva wasn't overjoyed about yet another house move, and she didn't like Berlin. So to begin with, Albert went off alone, ahead of the rest of the family.

To be honest, it wasn't just removals and Berlin that Mileva was unhappy about.

'Albert is tirelessly working on his (physics) problems,' she wrote to a friend. 'One can say that he lives only for them.' Once upon a time they'd shared everything, from books to dreams of the future.

Now the spark seemed to have gone out. Albert was too madly in love with physics to love Mileva too.

We used to be so close. Now he's on another planet!

All Albert's work was aimed at **a single goal**: to dream up a 'General Theory', one that, as far as possible, explained how everything worked all the time. This seemed a very big ask. Professor Planck told Albert:

As an older friend I must advise you against it, for in the first place you will not succeed; and even if you do succeed, no one will believe you!

Albert was still a rebel, though. Friends might tell him his imagination was just running away with him, but for Albert himself a big ask demanded a big answer!

On he went with his project – burning the candle at both ends – and this was the particular problem he was trying to crack:

- 💡 Isaac Newton had made it clear that gravity draws all objects towards one another, makes things fall to Earth and makes the planets go round and round.

- 💡 What Albert couldn't understand was how objects that were so far apart could affect one another. How did the Earth attract the Moon, for example?

Shall we dance?

- 💡 Was there something out there in space that carried the force between the two bodies – like the electromagnetic field that carries electromagnetic forces? Could there also be a `gravitational' field?

Gotcha!

For ten long and often manic years after 1905, Albert put his imagination into overdrive to get to the bottom of this. (Scientific breakthroughs hardly ever happen with a sudden 'light-bulb' moment.) He didn't just go blue in the face with all his imagining, he went a very deep shade of purple! But if there *was* a gravitational field, what kind of maths might describe it? Albert was having such difficulty working this out that, once again in his time of need, **he sent out a desperate message** to Marcel, his genius number-crunching friend from Zurich:

Marcel got to work, and finally, in 1915, Albert hit on a solution.

And here he is now to share it with you!

ALBERT EXPLAINS: WHAT SPACE REALLY IS

> Newton reckoned space was just a great empty container for the universe.
>
> In this container, everything runs in straight lines until a force makes those lines curve.

> The force is strong in me! Please go round.
>
> Righto!

But instead of this space being nothing at all, I wondered if it might be something. And if so, what sort of something? Now here – after long hard years of thinking and talking and violin-playing and pulling out my hair (which didn't matter too much because I had an awful lot of it!) – is the answer I came up with:

SPACE ACTUALLY IS THE GRAVITATIONAL FIELD! AND THE GRAVITATIONAL FIELD ACTUALLY IS SPACE!

"For Newton, space was flat and fixed. But I saw space as moving and bending, like a living thing – a field that shifts and sways . . ."

"And what makes space bend? Objects do. Especially massive objects like the Sun."

2,000,000,000,000,000,000,000,000,000,000 kg

The Sun warps space around itself.

But, it's not only space that has been warped, but 'spacetime' (see p. 64).

When the Earth and other planets circle the Sun, they're just following grooves mapped out by space that has been warped.

"My equation showed that spacetime curves in the neighbourhood of a star."

And because of this curving, light is made to change direction too.

> My equation also predicted that at a certain time, the Sun would cause light to change direction by a certain amount, and that this amount could not only be observed, it could be measured.

> And it's not just space that curves: time also shrinks or expands, depending on how close it is to objects. The Earth (a huge object) slows down spacetime slightly. So the closer you are to the ground, the slower time passes!

Imagine a pair of twins. At birth they are separated. One grows up in the hills, the other on the coast. When they meet years later, the twin from the hills will have aged a tiny bit more. If one twin lived just 12 inches (30 cm) higher up than the other for 79 years, she would be 90 billionths of a second older!

> I've got one more wrinkle than you!

That, then, was my General Theory. And in 1915 I let the world in on it.

The World Descends Into War

Not everyone immediately understood Albert's new theory. But those who did were stunned.

It seemed as if it might be **a totally different** way of looking at reality. But some people doubted Albert and in some ways they were right. No scientific theory can ever be proved absolutely correct. Not forever and a day. If that was the case, we'd still believe the Earth is flat! So everything always has to be up for grabs, in case new information comes to light. Albert knew this very well.

In 1915 he didn't think he had proved Newton 'wrong'. He was just making adjustments to Newton's ideas. And he fully expected that one day some other scientist would come along and make adjustments to his own adjustments!

But Albert's theory was still no more than an idea. Now his equation had to be tested, to see if it was right. And for that, **he needed an eclipse** of the Sun, and those don't happen very often.

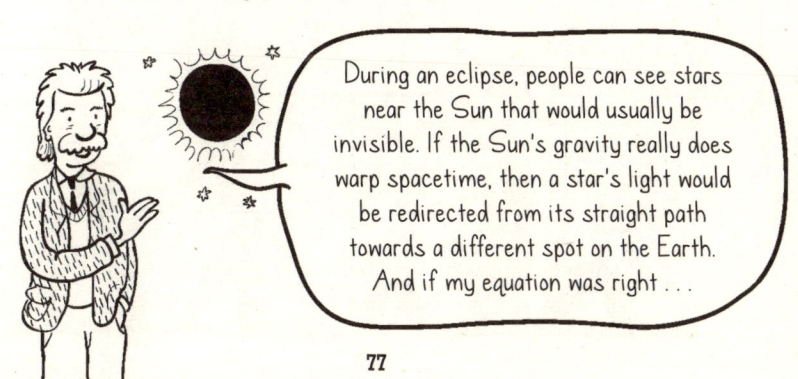

> During an eclipse, people can see stars near the Sun that would usually be invisible. If the Sun's gravity really does warp spacetime, then a star's light would be redirected from its straight path towards a different spot on the Earth. And if my equation was right . . .

*That's degrees as in a circle, not degrees as in Celsius!

Albert had already tried the test once, during an eclipse of the Sun that took place in August 1914. Eclipses are easier to photograph in some parts of the world than in others and organizing a mission to get those photos would cost a lot of money. But enough donations came in to finance a German expedition, which set out for Russia to make the observations and calculations. It ended in disaster. The scientific party was captured by the Russian army, and **all their equipment was confiscated**. Why on earth would the Russians be interested in a load of German scientists? Well, for a very good reason – three weeks earlier, Germany and Russia had gone to war with each other!

In fact, this was the start of the First World War – and neither Albert nor anyone else could know that it would last almost until that next eclipse, shockingly claiming almost *20 million* lives.

As the war dragged on and on, you can imagine Albert's horror. The mere thought of war used to give him the jitters. He hated confrontation so much that he **didn't even like playing chess**! The war didn't much affect his own daily life in Berlin, but now that he was starting to make a name for himself, he felt he had a duty to speak out about things that weren't strictly to do with science, and he started by signing an anti-war manifesto, then calling for a United States of Europe.

> I thought it was worth a try; people might just listen.

The End Of The Road For Johnnie And Dollie

As much as Albert believed in peace, he couldn't stop the struggle going on in his own home. Albert and Mileva had long since stopped being lovestruck Johnnie and Dollie. While once they'd found it impossible to live apart, by 1914 they decided they couldn't live together any more, and Mileva moved from Berlin back to Zurich with the children. Albert **cried all that afternoon and evening**. It was a terribly sad time for everyone.

Albert still got to see his boys, but meeting up was tricky now they lived in different countries. Even after the war was over, he didn't see them all that often. He did make sure his family never went hungry, though, and he promised Mileva a share in a kind of windfall one day. Every year, a committee in Sweden handed out the world's biggest and most valuable science awards, including the Nobel Prize in Physics. Albert said that when he won it, the prize money could be used by his sons and Mileva. *When* he won it, you'll notice, not *if*. Albert had always been confident. Some people (like his old teachers) might even have said he was a wee bit cocky.

'*The role as the wife of a genius is never easy*', said Albert's best friend Michele Besso. It truly must have been tough to live with Albert, who gave all his attention to tiny things like atoms, or vast things like galaxies, and very rarely to in-between-sized things like soap or dustpans and brushes or even other human beings!

But how would he manage all on his own in Berlin?

Well, maybe he wasn't completely alone . . . The truth was, Albert had already met another woman. Or rather, he'd reconnected with someone from his childhood. Elsa Löwenthal was his older cousin, related to him on both sides of his family. Now divorced and with two daughters of her own, Elsa also lived in Berlin – and even before Albert's marriage ended, they'd got talking.

Albert didn't fall head over heels for Elsa the way he had with Mileva, but they did grow very fond of each other, and Elsa made sure her 'Albertle' had perfect conditions to work in, with no outside distractions – which Albert liked very much. She'd even lay on a spread of Albert's favourite food (lentil soup and sausages) then **let him eat it all on his own** while he kept on thinking about the universe.

> Do you have an appointment to see the professor?
>
> I only came to ask if he'd keep the noise down.

Elsa **wasn't at all interested in science or maths**, except when it came to household bills, and she wasn't having any of Albert's more dodgy personal habits. She made sure he washed more often, and wore trousers that reached all the way down to his shoes.

> You are NOT going out looking like that!

They were more like brother and sister than madly in love, nevertheless Elsa became Albert's second wife in 1919. Soon, a third member of the Einstein clan joined the household – Albert's mum (who was also Elsa's aunt), the lady who decades earlier had got her son into music, and had probably always known he was a genius.

Sadly, though, she died of stomach cancer shortly after moving in. Albert couldn't keep a lid on his emotions. He wrote to a friend that he felt the loss right into his bones. But despite this deep sadness, at the age of 40, Albert was about to find lasting joy through his work.

Albert Joins The All-Time Greats

The year 1919 was going to be Albert's biggest yet. As you'll probably remember from p. 78 it was the year of **the next solar eclipse**, and on 29th May, Albert's General Theory of Relativity could finally be tested.

Not just one expedition but two had to be organized, to make sure all the right observations were made, and that took a lot of planning. Even before the First World War was over, a British scientific expedition was arranging to travel out to an island in the Atlantic Ocean off the coast of Africa, and also to Brazil.

As Professor Einstein says:

Science is the property of all nations and is not in any way endangered by international strife, for it always has a healing influence on those people who look beyond the horizon!

Sir Arthur Eddington

That's very nice, but can you give us a hand?

Seeing as Britain was still fighting against Albert's Germany at the time, this collaboration really was quite amazing!

By the time the expedition set off, the war had actually ended. But then – wouldn't you know it? – the weather conditions on eclipse day were all wet and cloudy, so for a while it looked as if the photos wouldn't come out clearly enough. And even when they did, it then took another *four months* for the results to be properly analysed.

So had Albert got it right? Like everyone else in the science world, he just had to wait and see. In the meantime, he swore blind he wasn't chewing up the carpet!

Finally, in September, the verdict reached Berlin. The science world held its breath. But Albert's prediction, based on his General Theory of Relativity, had been . . . accurate!

Spacetime Curves!

Put at its simplest, this was the vision Albert had struggled for like a demon. Then he had put his vision into equations, so that every other scientist could share it. There was no going back now – it was clear that Albert Einstein's theories explained how the universe worked **more fully than Isaac Newton's laws**! Tributes flooded in at once from all the top scientists who got this message loud and clear. One German physicist called the General Theory *'a great work of art'*!

And when Albert's old mates at the Olympia Academy back in Zurich (see p. 47) got to hear, they sent him a poem:

All doubts have now been spent
At last it has been found:
Light is naturally bent
To Einstein's great renown!

Albert celebrated his success by **buying himself a new violin**, and later – a little tongue-in-cheek – he asked Newton to forgive him.

But it didn't end there.

Albert's great breakthrough would pave the way for plenty more discoveries – some long after he died – just the way that Newton's had. The General Theory truly was a gift that kept on giving. But back in 1919, with the First World War over at last, people everywhere were hoping for a brighter future. They'd endured so much misery – now they were ready for something or someone to really catch their imaginations.

Albert was their man. He was about to become the world's first mega-celebrity.

7   ALBERTMANIA!

He didn't become a total legend overnight, though.

It took a fair bit of time for the news to get through to people who weren't top scientists. And it had always been Albert's intention that ordinary people *should* understand his work – which was why he wrote a book just for them in 1916 called *Relativity: the Special and the General Theory*.

He'd sell even more with a snappier title.

He was so keen to make sure his book was easy to follow that he **read every page out loud** to Margot, his teenaged stepdaughter. This plan didn't entirely work. Every time Albert stopped and asked, 'Have you got that bit?' Margot always answered, 'Yes, Albert.' But when anyone else asked her she'd say:

I find the whole thing totally baffling!

Yet the book is still on sale today, so lots of readers probably *have* understood it!

'WHAT DOES IT ALL *MEAN*?'

Plenty of other writers tried to explain Albert's ideas too. By 1925 more than 600 books and articles about relativity had been published, but a lot of people were **still totally bamboozled**. And not just uneducated people, either.

In 1921 Albert crossed the Atlantic by ship with another great scientist, Chaim Weizmann. 'During the crossing, Einstein explained his theory to me every day,' said Weizmann, 'and by the time we arrived I was fully convinced that he really understands it!' Even super-brainy French novelist Marcel Proust couldn't make head or tail of what he read.

> *I do not understand a single word of his theories.*

As Albert's fame spread, his post bag ballooned with questions about his brilliant ideas, and with worldwide invitations to come and speak about them. When he accepted the invitations, people queued up in their thousands to hear him lecture, especially in the USA.

Even after Albert started speaking, they had to be patient. He spoke in German, so all questions and answers had to go through an interpreter.

> Please, Professor, describe for us Americans your theory in one sentence.

> *All of my life I have been trying to get it into one book, and **he** wants me to get it into one sentence!*

Interpreter

Albert was even invited to the White House to meet US president Warren G. Harding. (And, yes, Mr President freely admitted relativity stumped him too.)

It didn't seem to matter whether people understood Albert's work or not. With his dreamy look and twinkly eyes, **he managed to charm everyone** – they only had to be told he was a total genius, then take one look at him, and they believed it!

And whenever Albert was in town, there were usually plenty of chances to get to see him. His visits might be celebrated with a procession of over a hundred cars, led by a marching band (still not his favourite sort of music, but hey!) and flag wavers:

- In one US city 15,000 excited spectators lined the streets.
- Five hundred uniformed girls serenaded him when he arrived in San Diego, California.
- Inside a New York church he was introduced to a life-sized statue of himself.

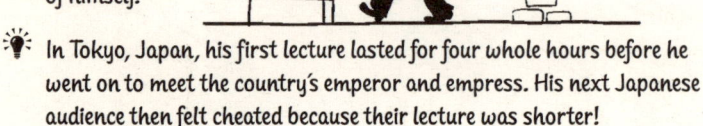

    Haven't we met before?

- In Tokyo, Japan, his first lecture lasted for four whole hours before he went on to meet the country's emperor and empress. His next Japanese audience then felt cheated because their lecture was shorter!

Pioneering scientists were not usually given this sort of treatment. Albert was more like a rock god on tour than a physicist!

In 1931, and by now a household name, he appeared at a movie premiere in Los Angeles, USA, alongside Hollywood star Charlie Chaplin. The crowds went wild.

They cheer me because they all understand me, and they cheer you because no one understands you.

Ach, but what does it all mean?

Nothing!

After all his struggles, Albert found this sort of hero worship pretty strange, but deep down he enjoyed most of the attention and pampering. He certainly didn't shy away from his new fans! Nor did Elsa, who travelled with him to all the places he was invited to speak. She even **made sure people paid** to get her Albertle's autograph or photo. She wasn't being greedy – all the money was donated to children's charities!

If it's a good theory, it should be possible to explain it to a child!

He must know some very clever children!

Albert really did enjoy getting to see so many other countries, but in these days before long-haul passenger flights, he adored even more the **lengthy ocean voyages** that took him there.

All that lovely time just to sit and think!

But with so many people now hanging on his every word, there was no way he could restrict himself to talking just about science. After years of using his imagination to find solutions, he now felt driven to use his fame to speak out about other issues that really mattered to him.

Outside of science, there were two things in particular that Albert felt the need to talk about. One was making sure no more world wars ever happened, and we'll be coming to that. The other was the way Jews were being treated in Europe . . .

GLOBETROTTING PRIZEWINNER

Crazily, after Germany lost the First World War, some Germans decided that the Jews were to blame and started picking on them as a result. This is a prejudice that's sometimes called anti-Semitism. Along with many other campaigners across the world, **Albert was outraged** at the treatment of his fellow Jews, but a plan was hatching that might just provide a solution:

Why not relocate many of Europe's Jews out of harm's way? They can be resettled back in Palestine.

We can start a new country of our own there!

Albert wasn't sure he liked the idea of separating Jews out, but he joined the campaign to create a new settlement in Palestine, and was especially keen to start a Jewish University in Jerusalem. He'd actually made his first tour of the USA in 1921 as part of a team trying to raise money to set up a new Jewish homeland. *'I am really doing whatever I can for the brothers of my race who are treated so badly everywhere,'* he told one crowd.

But back in Germany, anti-Semitism was getting out of hand – at home Albert wasn't quite such a pin-up. The police even warned him not to give any lectures in Berlin in case anti-Semitic fanatics – 'riff-raff' as Albert called them – **tried to bump him off**!

Albert wasn't exactly flavour of the month with the Nobel Prize committee, either. He'd had his first nomination for science's biggest annual award back in 1910! Despite 30 nominations since then, the award had always gone to someone else. It must have driven Albert mad wondering how long he would have to wait.

> No, no, really it didn't. Life's much too short for that sort of thing!

Too many scientists on the committee were experimental physicists, and they could be quite sniffy about theoretical physicists like Albert. Experimental physics was all about – well – experiments, observed and recorded in the lab, whereas Albert said he hardly dared pick up a piece of apparatus for fear it **might blow up**!

Zzz.

Anyone can just **think** things.

Ah, but it all depends on **what** you think.

NOBEL COMMITTEE

Not all physicists were completely convinced by relativity either. On the other hand, by the 1920s Albert was a superstar who had got the whole world talking about time and space and how the universe worked. So finally, after 14 top scientists nominated him, he pulled it off, winning the 1921 Nobel Prize for Physics! But he didn't win specifically for his work on relativity, he won it for discovering the Law of the Photoelectric Effect, one of the very first papers he'd written, in 1905!

Albert didn't seem to care. He didn't show up for the award ceremony in Sweden – he was on a speaking tour of Japan at the time (he loved it there) – and **didn't even mention the prize** in his diary on the day of the ceremony! There was, however, a kerfuffle about who should accept the prize on his behalf. Should it be the German ambassador or the Swiss ambassador? Albert still had both nationalities. In the end, the German ambassador 'won', but Albert was officially listed as being German *and* Swiss.

> Just call me a citizen of the world. This sort of 'national feeling' is the measles of mankind!

In that year, the prize was worth over 121,000 Swedish kronor – more than 12 times Albert's annual income, and more than 37 times what Mileva was living on each year! Because, of course, Albert had promised a share in this windfall to Mileva – which was really only fair, since she'd helped such a lot with his work in the early years and was bringing the boys up on her own. There was a bit of haggling, but that's hardly unusual between a divorced couple, and in the end **Albert stuck to his promise**. In later years the two of them managed to get along quite well, and when Albert travelled to South America, he even brought Mileva back some cactuses.

> It wasn't a joke; she really did like cactuses!

And to be honest, Albert wouldn't really miss that Nobel cash. As a result of his new-found fame, he wasn't making a fortune (and he never really would), but put it this way: he'd never have to worry about where his next meal was coming from.

Who's A Blockhead?

So now Albert was in a **pretty good place**.

He had truly made his mark and, thanks to his theories, people were thinking about the world in a whole new way. They were calling him the 'Father of Modern Physics', and it seemed his ideas really would help lots of younger scientists to make breakthroughs. But a new fear began to nag away at him: although he was still only in his forties, did he have anything more to give to the world of science?

*Anything truly novel is invented only during one's youth. Later one becomes more experienced, more famous and more **blockheaded**!*

Albert did have a point. He'd pushed hard for his early breakthroughs because he was such a rebel. No one in authority was going to tell *him* how the universe worked! Of course, he hadn't grown into a 'blockhead', but during the 1920s he was calling a lot of the shots himself. Who was he going to rebel against? In fact, as we'll soon see, although he was their hero, some of the younger physicists were threatening to rebel against *him*!

None of this was going to hold Albert Einstein back, though.

What he really longed to do was come up with an **even grander idea** – he called it a 'Unified Field Theory'. If he could just crack this one, he felt sure it'd help him to unlock every last secret of the universe.

> Ach, you want to talk about those pesky quanta again! They plagued me for so long! I was sure they had something vital to tell me.

So how about you explain what they are, Albert?

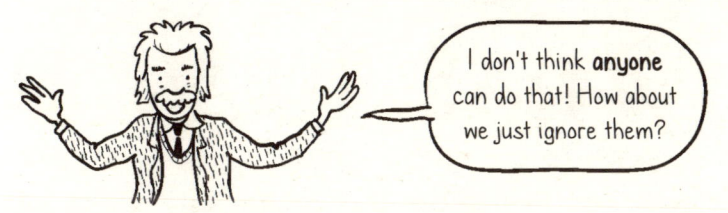

> I don't think **anyone** can do that! How about we just ignore them?

We-ell, you did spend nearly 40 years of your life trying to pin them down.

> You're right. So **you** do the explaining. And tell them about those young quantum guys too. I shall go and have a cigar.

Here Come The Quantum Guys

Niels Bohr was a Danish physicist, a bit younger than Albert and a great fan of his work. They got to meet and became true friends, even though they didn't spend much time agreeing with one another. In fact, they had **completely different views** on life, the universe and just about everything.

Once, when Albert visited Niels in Copenhagen, they got into such a debate in the tram, they missed their stop. They got off, travelled back, picked up their conversation – and missed the stop again!

They might know their way around the universe, but they can't find their way home!

Albert's 'pesky quanta' lay at the heart of their arguments. Remember they're the tiny grains of energy Albert described in his Law of the Photoelectric Effect? (A single grain, by the way, is called a quantum.) Now Niels and some other super-smart young scientists had dreamed up a brilliant new quantum theory.

This new generation of physicists was working out a system they called quantum mechanics.

For these guys, quanta seemed to be the building blocks of everything – yet it was pretty well impossible ever to predict what quanta were going to do next. Which led them to think that everything in life must be pretty random too. Albert thought their idea was fine as far as it went, but to him something still wasn't right.

He couldn't get his head around a kind of reality where *anything* could happen. *'It does not really bring us any closer to the secrets of God,'* he wrote. *'I, at any rate, am convinced that He does not play dice.'* When his friend Niels heard that, he said, 'Einstein, stop telling God what to do!'

Albert and the quantum team never did get to see eye to eye. Albert wanted **rules, not randomness** – ideally rules he'd discovered for himself! He never really worked as part of a team. Now he soldiered on alone, working around the clock to link together electricity, magnetism, gravity and quantum mechanics once and for all.

He was inspired by what Isaac Newton once wrote, *'Nature is pleased with simplicity'*. The best things in life for Albert – Mozart's music, the joys of hiking or sailing, lentil soup and sausages – were all quite simple and straightforward. So why shouldn't the design of the universe be marvellously simple too?

The trouble was: *explaining* this 'simple' design could turn out to be very complicated. At the end of January 1929, Albert published his latest attempt at an explanation – featuring 33 quite tricky equations – and **thousands of copies were sold**. One London department store even pasted up a set of the pages in its shop window.

I think I can follow it as far as the bottom of page two . . .

Is this the queue for the sofa sale?

But Albert's fellow physicists weren't convinced. On second thoughts, Albert wasn't either. He agreed that his workings still left room for improvement.

So back to the drawing board he went. This was frustrating, but actually the drawing board was the place where Albert most liked to be, with his magnificent brain still whirring away just as fast as it had when he was a small boy.

Albert Hits Fifty

In many ways life had turned out well for Albert. People everywhere just seemed to love him. On his 50th birthday, on 14th March 1929, strangers all over the world bombarded him with gifts and cards. An unemployed man sent a few coins he'd saved so Albert could buy himself a small packet of tobacco for his pipe. Albert wrote to thank him with tears in his eyes.

In truth, he didn't need much money to get by – he'd never be one to splash out on pointless luxuries – and **he had everything he needed**. His jobs in Berlin paid him well, he got fees for his overseas lecture tours and royalty payments for the books he wrote – and whenever he fancied a trip anywhere, he had countless open invitations to go and make speeches or attend conferences, all expenses paid! He really had become a citizen of the world.

'Life is like riding a bicycle,' he wrote to his son Tete. *'To keep your balance you must keep moving.'* At the age of 50, Albert was the world's least likely person to stop moving. His thoughts raced all day long (and probably all night too – in his dreams).

He liked nothing better than imagining away while sailing on a lake outside Berlin, where he, Elsa and her daughters had been able to buy a small summer house. For hours he'd drift alone on the water, even though he never learned to swim (or drive).

> Way too complicated!

Albert was still thinking about more than just science, though.

> Now that I had a voice in the world, you see, I wanted to speak up for those who didn't. The world's underdogs. I was once an underdog myself, so I knew all about that!

Science would always be Albert's first love, but speaking his mind on important world issues came a close second, and as the 1920s ended he saw **serious trouble looming** on the horizon. But speaking out now was going to cost him dear . . .

8   Albert Against The Nazis

At the end of 1930 Albert went on his second trip to America, although he and Elsa almost didn't make the boat after he **lost their train tickets** at the railway station in Berlin!

Albert was pleased to be back, but he was a deeply troubled man. In both Europe and the USA times were hard – millions of people were struggling to make ends meet, and their governments didn't seem to know how to help. The First World War had been called the war to end all wars, but now these governments still seemed awfully keen on training up soldiers.

Wherever Albert went, he was **mobbed by adoring fans**, and whenever he spoke to them, he seldom stuck to atoms and universes. He urged young men to refuse to do military service for their countries, even if they risked being sent to jail. He pointed out that the more men said no, the harder it would be to imprison them all. If even just two per cent said no, Albert declared in New York, governments would have to think again.

The idea of 'two per cent' seemed really cool to students and other peace campaigners, or 'pacifists', and they turned it into a catchphrase. Others happily chanted 'No War For Ever' when Albert came to speak, and a Youth Peace Federation was formed.

But the authorities in the USA and Europe kept a suspicious eye on him.

The Nazi Nightmare Begins

By 1932, Albert's fears for the future had deepened. The world seemed a desperately dangerous place, as country after country slumped into a **great economic depression**. Albert knew that at tense times like this, wars were all too likely to break out, so he started a campaign to set up a mighty international organization that would settle any arguments and 'enforce' peace. At the same time he urged all countries' governments to agree to 'disarm', or hand over their destructive weapons. There was only one sort of fight Albert was interested in – the fight for freedom!

> Our fight had to be against war itself! If war was eliminated, we'd all be free to think, imagine, create. Who knew what discoveries might follow!

It sounded great, but sadly for everyone, no such organization was ever set up, no countries disarmed – and, almost unbelievably, the sinister threat of a **second horrific world war** began to loom. Nowhere did that threat seem greater than in Albert's homeland.

While Albert was away from Germany, he was often asked what he thought of Adolf Hitler, who was leader of the National Socialist German Workers Party (Nazis for short). Hitler's plan, if the Nazis ever got into power, was to conquer and rule a new German empire or reich. These Nazis weren't exactly inclusive. They'd made it clear Jews would be treated as second-class citizens in their empire, yet plenty of struggling German citizens didn't seem to mind that. Naturally, Albert wasn't one of them. 'As soon as economic conditions improve,' he'd say in answer to the Hitler question, 'he will no longer be important.'

Economic conditions didn't get any better, however, and sometimes the Jews were blamed for this too. Then, in early 1933, the Nazis took power in Germany.

Albert was in the USA at the time, but on his return

voyage he got some shocking news. For no good reason at all, the Nazis had ransacked his study in Berlin, and raided his summer cottage. (They even came back later and **confiscated his boat**, in case Albert used it for 'smuggling'!)

Utterly unthinkable things were happening all over Germany. Soon books declared to be 'un-German' (many of them Jewish) were being thrown on to bonfires. One friendly German official pleaded with Albert not to go back or 'they'll drag you through the streets by the hair'. A Nazi magazine put a picture of Albert on its cover with the caption, 'Not Yet Hanged'. Rumours said that they had put a price of $5,000 (about $100,000 today) on his head!

I didn't know it was worth that much!

Maybe if you tidied it up a bit?

Albert was always quick to make a joke, but inside he must have been sickened.

ALBERT THE CELEBRITY REFUGEE

Jewish people were rushing to get out of Germany for good. They didn't feel they had a choice. Just having a Jewish grandparent was enough to lose a university lecturer his job. The country had to wave goodbye to no fewer than 14 Nobel Prize-winners! Germany had a total of 60 professors of theoretical physics; 26 of them felt forced to leave. **Hitler couldn't have cared less**.

With a heavy heart, Albert gave up his German citizenship for a second time. There was no way he and Elsa could stay. But where would they go instead?

Plenty of European universities would have welcomed Albert, and for a few months he and Elsa toured the continent weighing up their options. By now he had many friends in high places – including the queen of Belgium, who liked to perform Mozart's duets with him! But in October 1933, Albert and Elsa set sail across the Atlantic once again, with Albert's secretary, Helen Dukas, and his assistant, Walther Mayer.

Albert's plan was to do his own well-paid research that winter at the Institute for Advanced Study in Princeton, not far from New York. Then he thought he might spend the following spring at Oxford University in England. Little did he know that at the age of 54, he was actually **saying farewell to Europe** for ever.

> I cannot live in a land where people are told what to think. We should be free to question everything!

But even from thousands of miles away, the Nazis would one day have an enormous effect upon Albert's life.

Yankee Doodle Albert

A desk or table, a chair, paper and pencils – that was all the office equipment Albert said he needed at the institute. Oh, and a large wastebasket, for throwing away all his mistakes! He now had to learn to **say such things in English** too, which was pretty tough at his age! He never lost his German accent.

It wasn't easy either for Albert and Elsa to be **separated from all their children** back in Europe. And they could hardly forget about what was going on in Germany. But when Albert wasn't working on a Unified Field Theory in his new office, there was plenty else to enjoy, especially with a salary of something like $15,000 (Albert had only asked for $3,000!).

'*The whole of Princeton is one great park with wonderful trees,*' Elsa wrote to a friend from their rented home. Albert found some musicians he could play with; there was even a lake where he could sail his 17-foot (five-metre) wooden boat, *Tinef*, which means 'piece of junk' in the Jews' Yiddish language.

By 1935 they decided to make Princeton their permanent base, and set up home at 112 Mercer Street. It wasn't a very grand house, but it suited Albert perfectly – along with a parrot, a cat and a white terrier called Chico. Once the address got out, people all over the world deluged their hero with fan mail.

The dog is very smart. He feels sorry for me because I receive so much mail. That's why he tries to bite the mailman.

Soon Albert became a much-loved, scruffy and sockless local figure. Neighbours often saw him rambling around, lost in thought. Sometimes **local schoolkids dropped by** his house to ask for help with maths problems. Just as his old uncle Jakob had helped him, Albert showed the kids what needed to be done, then got them to work out the answers for themselves. But his memory was getting even worse.

One day, a secretary at the institute where he worked received a call from a stranger:

Can I help you?

Could you please give me Albert Einstein's home address?

I'm sorry, sir, we can't give out that information.

Ach, please don't tell this to anyone, but I **am** Professor Einstein. I'm on my way home, but I've forgotten where my house is!

Fresh Heartbreak

Not long after moving into Mercer Street, however, Elsa fell ill with heart and kidney problems, and she never really recovered. In December 1936 she died. Her Albertle was **ashen with grief**. The only way he could go on was by working harder than ever in his quest for a Unified Field Theory.

He told a colleague, '*I live like a bear in my cave.*' But he wasn't alone for long. In 1938 his beloved sister Maja came to share his cave. She'd been living in Italy, but life was getting as difficult for Jewish people there as it was in Germany. Maja wasn't in the best of health either, but Albert managed to sort out one nagging problem for her:

I'm a vegetarian, but I do so love hot dogs.

Then I hereby declare that hot dogs are vegetables!

He's a genius!

Albert's elder son, Hans Albert, was grown-up now, and worked as an engineer in Switzerland.

Albert hadn't seen much of him since he'd split up with Mileva but, nervous of what was going on in next-door Nazi Germany, he encouraged Hans Albert and his family to move to the USA too. With both men at least in the same country, they finally got to see a little more of each other.

Albert thought ***everyone*** **should be wary** of the Nazis. For five years they had been getting Germany ready for war. (How else could they carry out their plan to build an empire?) Yet in a 1939 survey to find the 'greatest living person', new students at Princeton University put Hitler top of the poll (Albert came second)!

That's a silver medal they can keep.

Finally, in September 1939, all Albert's deepest fears came true. The Nazis – soon to join forces with the war-mongering rulers of Italy and Japan – invaded neighbouring Poland, launching the **savage conflict** that spread around the globe and turned into the Second World War.

Albert was aghast. But he can't have been entirely surprised. Years earlier he had predicted: *'If and when war comes, Hitler will realize the harm he has done Germany by driving out the Jewish scientists.'*

We will never know whether Hitler realized it or not, but Albert was absolutely right; he really had shot himself in the foot!

THE ROAD TO MASS DESTRUCTION

After Albert had gone public with his General Theory in 1915, he'd met a young man who tried to explain an idea he'd had.

> Based on your $E=mc^2$ equation, people might find a way to unleash all the energy inside an atom to make terrifying explosives!

> Don't be foolish.

But by 1939 other physicists had found this idea wasn't foolish at all. Almost by accident they had discovered that **awesome amounts of energy** might come from 'splitting the atom'. This energy might then be used to make a bomb that was more massively destructive than any weapon known to man. (Remember that raisin back on page 66?)

No prizes for guessing how Albert felt when he was let in on this top-secret news.

> Professor, the Nazis might try to work out how to build this bomb. What if they succeed?

The man of peace was all in pieces. Here was Albert: a person in love with the harmony of the universe, a person who believed with all his heart that *'the murder of men is disgusting'*. Yet now his own brilliant discovery might be hijacked to create **the most murderous weapon of all**!

The discovery was not Albert's fault in any way, but he still felt a huge weight of responsibility. What in the name of spacetime was he to do now? He hated violence with every bone in his body, but a solution kept suggesting itself: the Nazis might think twice before dropping their atom bomb if they thought the Americans had built one of their own. On the other hand, maybe the Nazis *wouldn't* work out how to build one at all?

Round and round it all went in Albert's shaggy head. This was one of the **worst moments in his life**. He had never imagined he could get involved in weapon-building.

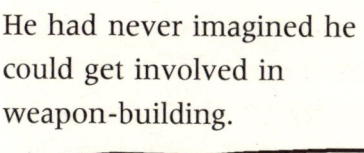

> But in science, when new facts arise, we have to rethink our ideas. In life we must do the same, though this can be so much harder.

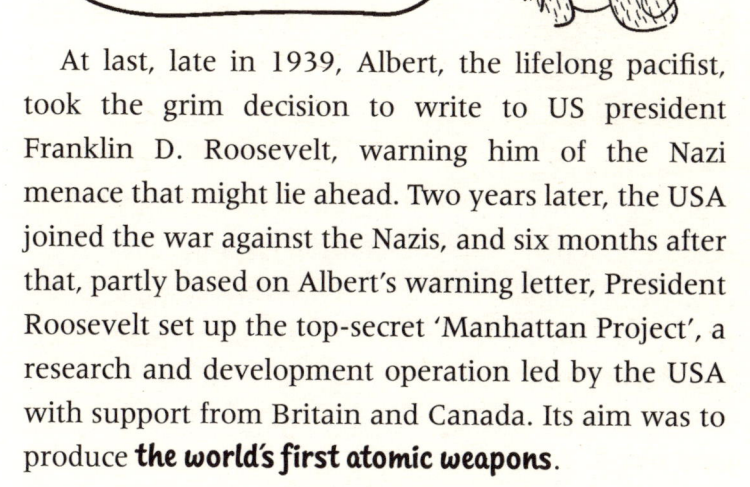

At last, late in 1939, Albert, the lifelong pacifist, took the grim decision to write to US president Franklin D. Roosevelt, warning him of the Nazi menace that might lie ahead. Two years later, the USA joined the war against the Nazis, and six months after that, partly based on Albert's warning letter, President Roosevelt set up the top-secret 'Manhattan Project', a research and development operation led by the USA with support from Britain and Canada. Its aim was to produce **the world's first atomic weapons**.

> If the Nazis beat us to it, there might not BE a world for very much longer!

In 1945 the USA won this dreadful race, creating the deadliest weapon the world had ever seen. If Hitler hadn't driven out so many brilliant Jewish physicists, the result might have been different. Many of the brains behind the Manhattan Project were Jewish. Some were refugees from Germany, though Albert himself wasn't among them. (He'd have helped out if needed, but the US authorities still **believed he couldn't be trusted**, even though in 1940, without giving up his Swiss citizenship, he'd officially become an American.)

By the time the bomb was ready, Hitler's Nazis had been defeated in Europe. The Einstein household didn't celebrate much, as hellish news soon followed: the Nazis had murdered six million European Jews, men, women and children, in what came to be known as the Holocaust. Albert's cousin Roberto – the son of his uncle Jakob – wrote to Albert telling him how his own wife and two daughters had been killed in cold blood. Soon afterwards, unable to live with the torment, Roberto Einstein killed himself.

Meanwhile, Japan's leaders were still refusing to give themselves up, and the idea grew that the US might drop atomic bombs on its cities to force them to surrender. The thought chilled Albert to the core. Since his first visits to the country, he'd always had a very soft spot for the Japanese, although he'd have felt equally horrified on behalf of any people anywhere on Earth. Again Albert wrote to the president, hoping catastrophe might still be avoided.

But soon, all his hopes were dashed. In August 1945, in a last-ditch bid to end the war, US planes dropped atomic bombs on the Japanese cities of Hiroshima and Nagasaki. The result was almost unimaginable carnage.

The first bomb alone killed 80,000 people instantly, and wiped out nearly five square miles of the city. When Helen Dukas broke the news to Albert, he was **too stunned to say anything** except, 'Oh, my God.' Later, though, as the full horror sank in, he bitterly regretted how his own scientific breakthroughs had been turned to such cataclysmic ends:

If I knew they were going to do this, I would have become a shoemaker.

The bombs did force the Japanese to surrender, and peace was restored to the world at last. But atomic bombs were here to stay, and Albert knew all too well the threat they posed to everyone. *As long as there will be man*, he said, *there will be war.*

Before long other countries would want their own atomic bombs – and if atomic war broke out, the whole planet might be **blown to bits**!

Albert was now a widower of 66, and his old stomach problems from 30 years before hadn't gone away. He had made so many massive contributions to science, no one would have minded if he finally started taking things easy.

But this was Albert Einstein. He lived to work, and he was still beavering away in his quest to find a Unified Field Theory, but for the next decade he gave himself an extra, unpaid job. Still disgusted by the hijacking of his own scientific ideas, he made a decision: he would use his fame to help to save the human race!

9   Albert Stays Awestruck

When the Second World War ended in 1945, America, Russia and Britain were the three **mightiest countries on Earth**. It wasn't long before the Russian and American 'superpowers' started getting twitchy, and accusing each other of making plans for world domination.

Things got even twitchier when the Russians began to build their own atomic weapons. Wearily Albert shook his head; he had seen all this coming. The United Nations was set up in 1945 to try to keep countries friendly. But Albert had an idea that was much bigger and bolder: he didn't just want to abolish all weapons of mass destruction across the world, he pretty much wanted to make borders between countries disappear too.

He came up with a simple plan:

1. The Americans, Russians and British could set up a world government right away.

2. They could invite other nations to join them.

3. This government could have its own armies to bring peace if war broke out anywhere in the world.

There really wasn't any time to lose, Albert warned anyone who cared to listen, because the next world war could only get a whole lot nastier.

> *I don't know how the Third World War will be fought, but I can tell you what they will use in the fourth – rocks.*

Chairman, Emergency Committee of Atomic Scientists

There weren't many smarter guys around than Albert, so you'd have thought his plan would be taken seriously. But it didn't get a particularly warm welcome, especially from Americans who felt Albert should be putting the USA first. And besides, getting people to think in new ways is always hard. Many Americans truly believed the Russians were the enemy – and if Albert didn't agree with them, well, **he must be an enemy** too!

> He's not even from the US.

> That makes him an alien!

> Maybe he's a Russian spy!

Albert had once been just about the most popular foreigner in the USA. Not any more. Some people really did believe he was a **threat to national security** – Albert could hardly believe it.

The USA's top security service, the Federal Bureau of Investigation (FBI), was worried enough to put together a file on him. And when Albert spoke up in favour of others in America who didn't seem to hate Russians either, the mood got ugly.

STICK TO THE STARS MR WISE GUY!

Go Home Professor!

BUTT OUT ALBERT!

Hands Off Our Bomb!

Despite your great scientific knowledge, you are an idiot, a menace to this country.

CHICAGO DAILY TRIBUNE
It is always astonishing to find that a man of great intellectual power in some directions is a simpleton or even a jackass in others.

So much for being the world's first mega-celebrity!

The FBI's file on Albert totted up in the end to 1,427 pages, stored in 14 separate boxes marked 'Confidential'. And what did they say? Well, it turns out that there wasn't a scrap of incriminating evidence! Lots of the information was simply wrong, like saying Albert had only one son, while most of the rest was empty gossip. He was not a spy, he wasn't a traitor to his new homeland – he was just desperately trying to find a way to **stop mankind exterminating itself**.

Another Explosive Situation

But Albert's wise advice wasn't being ignored just in the USA.

Over in Palestine in 1948, a new country called Israel was created. Jews had lived in this area thousands of years before and now – having suffered so terribly during the Second World War – large numbers of them were officially able to move back.

Albert had never been too sure about this plan. He'd visited Palestine himself in 1923, and found that thousands of Jews – about 86,000, in fact – had already settled there. That was fine. But more than 500,000 other people were living there too – most of them were Arabs, whose roots in the region were just as deep.

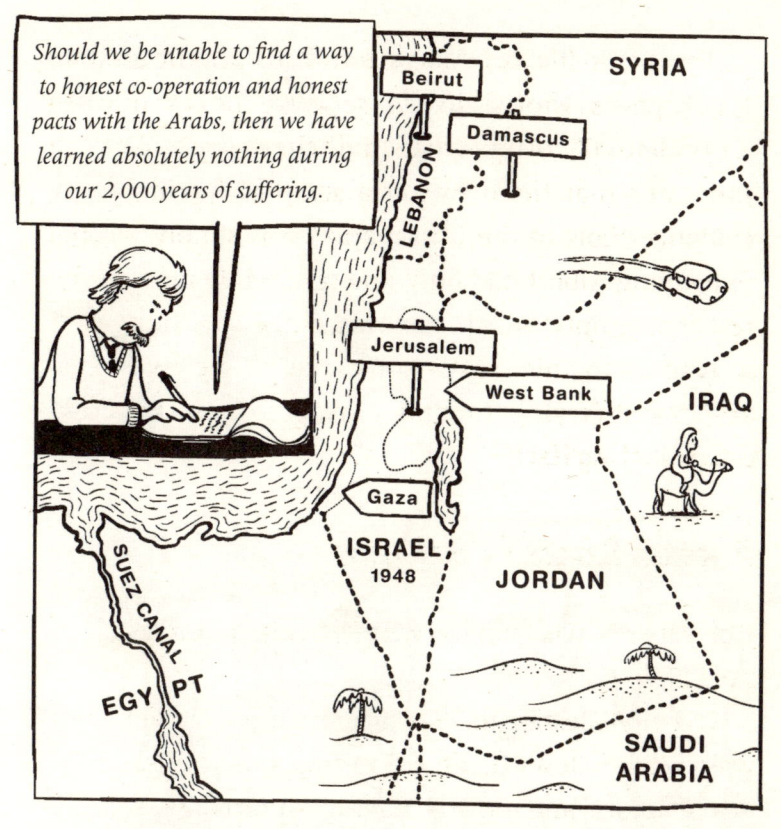

Albert wanted Jews and Arabs to try living together in a shared country – but it was not to be. The new Israel had borders and an army like any other country and, not surprisingly, a series of wars between Arabs and Israelis soon began.

Yet, in 1952, when Israel's first president died, guess who was invited to head up the new country, in spite of his views? That's right – the post was offered to the **world's most famous** Jewish person: Albert!

He would have been more of a figurehead than anything and they'd have been happy for him to carry on with his scientific research. Albert said it was nice of them to ask, but at the age of 73 he didn't really fancy moving to the Middle East and becoming a citizen of yet another country. So his answer had to be a polite no.

> Maybe it's no bad thing. I mean: a sockless head of state?

Israeli ambassador

THE THINKING FINALLY STOPS

Albert had planned to fully retire when he turned 66 in 1945 – but his birthday came and went, and nothing could keep him away from his small office at the institute. There was work to do! That Unified Field Theory wasn't going to discover itself!

Day in, day out, he'd have breakfast, then amble up Mercer Street in his baggy sweatshirt and corduroy trousers, thinking as hard as ever. He rarely turned to his violin for inspiration these days; it was hard to play with fingers stiffened by age. And no more Big Answers came his way. In the end, he accepted that the General Theory was his crowning achievement, and in 1951 he said he was 'retiring' his quest for a Unified Field Theory.

He carried on discussing smaller physics problems, which were still tricky enough, with colleagues who number-crunched equations for him, and sometimes he'd break off and say:

I will a little t'ink.

Then he'd stride up and down in silence, playing with his great mop of hair, till at last he came up with an answer. And for a while his sad old eyes would light up.

For 70 years since he'd held that compass as a little boy in Germany, Albert had **never lost his sense of wonder**. He was still just as awestruck about the heavens and the Earth and the great questions of life – maybe even more so, now his life was almost over.

By 1955 Albert was not a well man. For seven years his doctors had known that a blood vessel close to his heart was ballooning up dangerously. They did all they could to help, but it was clear the end was near.

Albert **wasn't afraid of death**, and when the blood vessel finally burst, his secretary Helen was the one who had to be comforted. Taking her face in his hands, he said calmly, *'I have to pass on sometime, and it doesn't really matter when.'*

Time had been smack in the centre of Albert's thinking for so long, and he'd changed the way that so many people understood it. Some even wondered if one day it would be possible to travel in time.

I was never convinced about that idea. But how I'd have loved to travel back in time, to start again, and have another crack at finding a Unified Field Theory!

On Monday 18th April 1955 Albert died.

He'd been using his incomparable imagination right up to the end. By his hospital bedside were papers covered with his most recent calculations. There was also a copy of a speech he'd been planning to give in Israel. It began:

I speak to you today not as an American citizen and not as a Jew, but as a human being...

One of history's greatest human beings was no more. He'd been called the 'Dopey One', and written off as a rebel, but in the end the man who'd looked beyond the horizon for the whole of his life became a true citizen of the world.

Albert hadn't wanted a big funeral with lots of fuss, so his ashes were scattered before most people even knew he'd died. But part of his body never made it to the crematorium. The morning after his death, a school teacher in Princeton asked her fifth-grade class what was in the news.

The schoolboy was telling the truth. His dad, Thomas Harvey, was a doctor at Albert's hospital. He'd been given the job of checking over the major organs in Albert's dead body; this included **cutting through the skull** with an electric saw, so he could inspect the brain. But then he decided to **pickle that bit of Albert** and keep it for scientific research! He hadn't asked anyone's permission. Albert's relatives had no idea.

No doctor would ever get away with that today, but for the next *43 years* Harvey passed out small chunks of Albert's brilliant brain for analysis! Was the grey matter of a genius different from everyone else's? No one has ever been able to say.

I could have told them they wouldn't find anything. It was a no-brainer!

THE FUTURE IS ALBERT-SHAPED

When news of Albert's death went public, US president Dwight Eisenhower led heartfelt tributes that flooded in from all over the world. *'No other man,'* he said, *'contributed so much to the vast expansion of 20th-century knowledge.'* Back then, the 20th century had only just passed its halfway point, but four and a half decades later that verdict still hadn't changed. On 31st December 1999 Albert was voted 'Person of the Century' in *Time* magazine.

Albert was gone, but his ideas lived on. Most importantly – and just as he would have hoped – his theories gave rise to yet more scientific discoveries:

- 💡 The laser was invented from work that Albert did on how large numbers of atoms interact with light.

- 💡 And have you heard of black holes? In Albert's time no one had. But his General Theory predicted them – and today we have the technology to spot and study them.

What are black holes?

They're stars that squash in on themselves so the space around them curves until it actually plunges down . . . er, a hole.

YIKES!

A black one.

Er, yup.

- 💡 We also now believe the universe emerged from a 'Big Bang' 14 billion years ago. In 1964, scientists discovered radiation left over from the terrific heat of that event. And whose theories had suggested this would turn out to be the case? Albert's!

- 💡 And how about this? Albert put his wonderful visions into equations. Now and then these equations seemed to suggest new visions of their own. Yet sometimes even Albert couldn't grasp what his phenomenal mind was telling him. According to his own calculations, the universe had to be constantly expanding. This seemed so incredible that for a few years Albert simply refused to believe it – but it was true, as modern research has proved.

Ach, so you see I could get things wrong too!

But you got so much *right*!

It's kind of you to say so. But still we need new ideas.

Well, maybe a genius of the future has just read this book? Maybe this story of the great Albert Einstein's life will inspire them to **rethink reality** one day, just the way you did?

> Then I wish them all the luck in the world! There are so many mysteries still to be solved! It is all about imagining what has not yet been imagined. That's why I always believed imagination was more important than knowledge, because knowledge has limits, but imagination can take you **anywhere**!

Timeline

I certainly asked a lot of questions!

14th March 1879   Albert is born.

1884   Albert holds a compass for the first time and his interest in the mysteries of Earth is sparked.

1894   Albert goes to Italy to escape doing military service.

1895   Albert takes the tests to get into Zurich Technical College two years early – and fails.

1896   Albert attends a secondary school in Switzerland, passes his diploma and then gets a place at Zurich Technical College.

1897   Albert meets and falls in love with Mileva Marić.

1890   Albert graduates from Zurich Technical College.

1901   Albert becomes a Swiss citizen.

1902   After months of struggling to find work, Albert takes a post at the Federal Office for Intellectual Property.

1903   Albert and Mileva can finally afford to get married.

1904   Albert's first son, Hans Einstein, is born.

1905   Albert's big year: he proves atoms exist and that light is made up of tiny particles, he comes up with his Special Theory of Relativity, AND his famous equation, $E=mc^2$.
On top of all that, he becomes Dr Einstein after completing his thesis on the size of molecules.

1910   A second son, Eduard Einstein (Tete), is born.

1911   Albert becomes Professor of Theoretical Physics at the German University in Prague.

1912   Albert becomes Professor of Theoretical Physics at the Federal Institute of Technology in Zurich.

1913   Albert becomes a German citizen again, so he can work as a professor at Berlin University (but he hangs on to his Swiss citizenship).

1914	Mileva, Hans and Eduard move from Berlin back to Zurich – without Albert.
1915	Albert shares his General Theory of Relativity.
1916	Albert's book *Relativity: the Special and the General Theory* is published.
1919	Albert marries his cousin, Elsa Löwenthal. A solar eclipse proves that his General Theory of Relativity is accurate.
1921	Albert wins the Nobel Prize for Physics. Hugely famous now for his theories, he accepts invitations to travel to the USA and most other parts of the world to speak about his brilliant ideas.
1933	The Nazis take power in Germany, where rumours spread that Albert is to be assassinated. Albert and Elsa leave permanently for America.
1936	Elsa dies.
1939	The Nazis invade Poland and the Second World War begins.
1940	Albert officially becomes an American citizen.
1945	In an effort to end the war, and to Albert's utter horror, US planes drop on Japan atomic bombs based on his $E=mc^2$ equation.
1951	Albert steps back from his quest to find a Unified Field Theory.
18th April 1955	Albert dies.
1999	Albert is voted Person of the Century in *Time* magazine.

Glossary

aerosol
A liquid that is held in a container under pressure and released in the form of a spray.

amber
Fossilized resin from a tree. It is usually yellow and often used to make jewellery or ornaments.

apparatus
Tools and equipment.

Arab
Someone who originally comes from the Arab world, which includes Arabia and other Middle Eastern countries.

atom
The tiniest possible part of a chemical element. Every solid, liquid and gas is made up of a collection of atoms.

botany
The scientific study of plants.

cataclysmic
Violent and catastrophic.

cosmic
Relating to the universe.

crematorium
A place where a dead person's body is burned to ashes.

diploma
A certificate awarded by a school, college or university.

electromagnetism
A branch of physics that studies the physical interaction between electrically charged particles.

engineering
The study of the design, building and use of engines, machines and structures.

equation
A mathematical statement where the figures on either side of the = sign have the same value.

evaporate
To turn from liquid into gas, e.g. puddles will dry up after rain because the warmth of the Sun causes the puddle water to evaporate.

federal
To do with the central government of a country.

galaxy
A collection of billions of stars, and other matter like gas and dust, held together by gravity. (Planet Earth is in the Milky Way galaxy.)

geometry
Maths relating to the study of the angles, points and lines of shapes and objects.

intellectual property
Inventions, designs and works of art – things that come from people's imaginations – are known as 'intellectual property' and can be protected by law.

magnetism
The force in and around a magnetic field that can attract objects or push them away (repel them).

manifesto
A document that sets out the beliefs and aims of an organization, especially a political party.

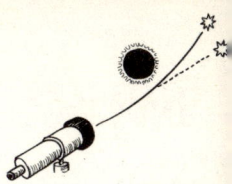

molecule
Two or more atoms bonded together. A molecule is the smallest unit any substance can be broken down into without changing its chemical make up.

orbit
To travel around something, e.g. the Earth takes one year to orbit the Sun.

particle
A tiny amount of a substance.

physicist
A scientist who deals with physics: the study of physical substances and energy.

prejudice
An opinion formed, e.g. before meeting someone, that isn't based on facts or experience, but on an idea (usually negative) of what that person is like.

radiation
Waves of energy sent out by light or heat sources.

rheumatism
A disease that causes swelling in muscles and joints, making the body become stiff and painful.

solar eclipse
When the Moon is positioned so that it blocks out the Sun's visible light for people watching on Earth.

think tank
A group of people who research and analyse complicated problems.

trillion
1,000,000,000,000! That's a million times a million.

twilight zone
An unclear or vague area between two places or conditions, which is neither one thing nor the other.

vibrate
To shake continuously and quickly.

zoology
The science and study of animals.

These are just a few of my favourite particles.

INDEX

Use these pages for a quick reference!

A

absent-mindedness 13, 17, 33, 46, 55, 110
Andromeda Galaxy 64
Arabs 122–3
atomic weapons 113–18, 119
atoms 48–9, 57–9
authority, attitude to 16, 18, 31, 96

B

Berlin 70, 79, 81, 93, 101, 106
Besso, Michele 47, 81
Big Bang 131
black holes 130
Bohr, Niels 98–9
brain, Albert's 9, 128–9
Brownian motion 58

C

Chaplin, Charlie 90
childhood 7–9, 12–20
children 45, 68–9, 80
colour vision 54
compasses 7–9, 19, 34
Copernicus, Nicolaus 50

D

death 127–30
Dirac, Paul 69
disarmament 104–5
doctorate 46, 67
Dukas, Helen 107, 117

E

$E=mc^2$ 65–6, 113
Earth
    and the Moon 72
    orbit of Sun 50, 62
    rotation of 62
    round vs. flat 48–9
    and spacetime 76
eclipses, solar 77–8, 83–4
Eddington, Arthur 83
education 16, 17, 21–6
Einstein, Eduard ('Tete') (son) 45, 68–9, 80, 95, 101
Einstein, Elsa (née Löwenthal) (2nd wife) 81–3, 91, 101, 107, 109, 111
Einstein, Hans Albert (son) 45, 68–9, 80, 95, 111–12
Einstein, Hermann (father) 7, 12–13, 21, 25, 36, 39, 45
Einstein, Jakob (uncle) 18, 21, 24, 110, 116
Einstein, Maja (sister) 12–13, 111
Einstein, Margot (stepdaughter) 87–8
Einstein, Pauline (mother) 12–13, 14, 25, 36, 39, 82–3
Einstein, Roberto (cousin) 116
Eisenhower, Dwight D. 129–30
electric forces 52–4, 99
electromagnetism 54–5, 64
energy 61, 66–7, 98, 113
exams 32, 37–8

F

fame 87–92
Faraday, Michael 53, 54, 55
Federal Bureau of Investigation (FBI) 121, 122
Federal Institute of Technology (Zurich) 68
fields
    electric and magnetic 53–4, 64, 72
    gravitational 72–3, 74
First World War 78–9, 83–4, 85, 92, 103
forces 52–4, 74

G

German University (Prague) 68
gravitational field 72, 73, 74
gravity 51, 72, 77, 99
Greeks, ancient 48–9, 53, 57
Grossmann, Marcel 32–3, 42, 73

H

Habicht, Conrad 44, 47
Haller, Mr 43–4
Harding, Warren G. 89
Harvey, Thomas 128–9
health problems 39, 118, 126–7
Hiroshima and Nagasaki 117
Hitler, Adolf 105, 107, 112, 113, 116
Holocaust 116

138

I

imagination 27–9, 71, 73, 132
Israel 123–4, 127

J

Japan 90, 94, 112, 116–17
Jews
    anti-Semitism 18–19, 38, 92, 93, 105–7, 111, 116
    new homeland for 92–3, 122–4
job applications 38, 42
job offers 68–9, 70

L

lasers 130
Laue, Max von 56–7
lecture tours 88–90, 94, 101
light
    direction of 75–6, 77
    speed of 28, 66
    waves and particles 60–1
light years 64

M

Mach, Ernst 58
magnetic forces 8, 19, 52–3, 99
Manhattan Project 115
Marić, Mileva (1st wife) 34–40, 44–5, 46, 47, 68, 70–1, 79–81, 95, 112
marriages 44, 82
mass 66
maths 18, 20, 26–7, 32, 51–2, 73
Maxwell, James Clerk 54, 55
Mayer, Walter 107
military service 16, 23, 26, 103–4
Milky Way 64
molecules 59, 60, 67
Moon 51, 72
Mozart, Wolfgang Amadeus 14, 15
Munich 7, 15, 22
music 14–15, 34, 82

N

nationality 23, 26, 39, 70, 95, 107, 116
Nazi regime 105–7, 108, 112–13, 114, 115, 116
Newton, Isaac 51, 72, 74, 75, 77, 84, 85, 99
Nobel Prize 80–1, 93–6

O

Olympia Academy 47, 85

P

pacifism 15–16, 79, 103–4, 114, 115, 119–20
Palestine 92–3, 122
particles 60–1
Patent Office 42–4, 47, 56, 67
Pavia, University of 23
Pernet, Jean 31
Photoelectric Effect, Law of the 60, 94, 98
physics 26–7, 31, 33, 46–7, 56–7
    new discoveries 40, 55
    theoretical 68, 93–4, 107
Planck, Max 56, 60–1, 71
planetary motion 72, 75
power generation 67
present time 63–4
Princeton 108, 109, 112
Proust, Marcel 88

Q

quanta/quantum physics 61, 97, 98–9

R

reality 48–9, 77
Relativity
    Albert's book about 87–8
    General Theory of 65, 71, 74–7, 83–6, 113, 125
    Special Theory of 61–5
Roosevelt, Franklin D. 115
Russia 119–20, 121

S

scientific papers 46–7, 56, 61, 65, 67, 68
scruffiness 17, 20, 57, 68, 82, 110
Second World War 112–17, 119
Solovine, Maurice 44, 47
space 10, 53, 55, 61, 74–6
spacetime 10, 64, 75–7
    curving of 75–6, 77, 84–5
Sun 50, 51, 75, 76, 77–8

T

Talmud, Max 18, 19–20, 22
thesis 67
thought experiments 27–9, 47
time 10, 55, 61, 63
twilight zone 64

U

Unified Field Theory 97–100, 109, 111, 118, 124–5
United Nations 119
United States
    Albert moves to 108–10, 116
    lecture tours 88–9, 103
    suspicion of Albert in 120–2
United States of Europe 79
universe 37, 40, 51, 64, 74, 97, 99, 131

V

vibrations 53–4
violin 14–15, 30, 68, 85, 125

W

waves, light 28, 35, 54, 60–1
Weber, Heinrich 31–2, 38, 40
wedding 44
Weizmann, Chaim 88
Winteler, Jost 25, 27
Winteler, Marie 33
women, education 34, 36

Z

Zurich Technical College 23–4, 25, 26, 30–2, 37
Zurich University 67, 68

There's so much to wonder about.

True life stories of the most amazing people EVER!

first names

Meet *Emmeline*

She's the feisty campaigner who fought a tough battle to win the vote for British women – and inspired thousands of others all over the world.

Emmeline PANKHURST
Haydn Kaye

Women WILL get the vote!

Ha! And men will walk on the moon!

Find out:

★ Why she said knickers to her bosses

★ Why she needed lessons in stone throwing

★ And why she was always on the run from the police

VOTES FOR WOMEN

Meet

Ada

She's the fast-thinking mathematician, who predicted the power of computers long before they were even invented.

first names

I dreamed up computer programming!

But computers don't even exist yet!

Ada
LOVELACE

Ben Jeapes
Illustrated by Nick Ward

Find out:

★ Why her mum kept her away from her mega-famous celebrity dad

★ Why she was mesmerized by memerism

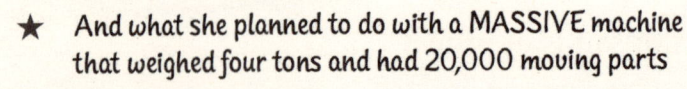

★ And what she planned to do with a MASSIVE machine that weighed four tons and had 20,000 moving parts

Get on **first name** terms with some of the world's most amazing people!

FICKLING
David Fickling Books